Wage and Price Controls

edited by
John Kraft
Blaine Roberts

The Praeger Special Studies program—utilizing the most modern and efficient book production techniques and a selective worldwide distribution network—makes available to the academic, government, and business communities significant, timely research in U.S. and international economic, social, and political development.

Wage and Price Controls
The U. S. Experiment

Praeger Publishers   New York   Washington   London

PRAEGER SPECIAL STUDIES IN U.S. ECONOMIC, SOCIAL, AND POLITICAL ISSUES

Library of Congress Cataloging in Publication Data
Main entry under title:

Wage and price controls.

(Praeger special studies in U. S. economic, social,
and political issues)
    Includes bibliographical references.
    1. Wage-price policy—United States—Addresses,
essays, lectures.   2. Price regulation—United States—
Addresses, essays, lectures.   I. Kraft, John.
II. Roberts, Blaine, 1944-
HC110. W24W33   338. 5'26'0973   74-30708
ISBN 0-275-05950-2

PRAEGER PUBLISHERS
111 Fourth Avenue, New York, N.Y. 10003, U.S.A.

Published in the United States of America in 1975
by Praeger Publishers, Inc.

Printed in the United States of America

In editing this book on the impact of wage and price controls in the United States, we established certain ground rules for the contributors and for the subject matter of the text. First, at least one contributor of each chapter had to have had some actual experience with the Economic Stabilization Program, either as a staff member of the Price Commission or the Cost of Living Council or as an advisor of these groups in either a public or private capacity. Second, the book had to include a mixture of econometric and noneconometric analysis of the impact of the wage and price controls; the econometric analysis of the program appears in Chapters 6, 7, 8, and 9. Third, the contributors had to consist of a heterogenous group including individuals favorable and unfavorable to controls. Last, the book would attempt to touch on all aspects of the program: the business viewpoint, the government viewpoint, prices, wages, administrative aspects, alternatives to controls, macroeconomic aspects, and the industrial impact of controls. Pressures, deadlines, and other commitments did not allow us to include contributions from as many individuals as we had hoped, but nevertheless we are able to present a group of essays that, with the exception of one, were all written expressly for this book. We would like to thank each contributor for the effort put forth.

Before moving to the text, it should be valuable to the reader for us to present the background for each chapter. Chapters 1 through 5 represent a less quantitative analysis of the program and thus are probably of more interest to the layman; Chapters 1, 2, and 3 focus on the price aspects of the wage and price controls program. Sidney L. Jones, in Chapter 1, comments on lessons ne learned from the program while he was Assistant Secretary of Commerce for Economic Affairs. Chapter 2 best represents the business view of price controls; during the period of controls the author, Jerry Pholm was a member of the Price Commission and Cost of Living Council, except during Phase IV, when he was an economist in the private sector. Professor Askin's chapter is a summary of many of the ins and outs of the birth of the price control apparatus and is a somewhat unique view of controls. The wage aspects of the Economic Stabilization Program are covered in Chapters 4 and 5. Chapter 4 analyzes the Pay Board and wage controls machinery of Phases II, III and IV, while Chapter 5 focuses on one particular aspect of the wage picture: escalation clauses. The econometric attempts at analyzing the program are presented in Chapters 6, 7, 8, and 9. Each of these chapters focuses on a particular aspect of the program. Chapter 6 compares wage and price controls against the use of tax policy. The stage-of-processing, industrial, and macro-economic impacts of the program are analyzed in Chapters 7, 8, and 9.

The book contains something for everyone, whether layman, professional economist, or technician. While the evidence presented in the text does not provide a solution to the controls controversy, it will provide the reader with insights into the workings of the program.

CONTENTS

LIST OF TABLES

Wage and Price Controls

1

THE LESSONS OF
WAGE AND PRICE
CONTROLS
Sidney L. Jones

From almost three years of experience it appears that we have learned a lot about wage and price controls but not how to control wages and prices. An even more important lesson is that monetary and fiscal policies must become more stable to moderate supply and demand distortions. The allocation of human and material resources is an exceedingly complex process in which prices determine relative values in the market system. Since August 15, 1971, the United States government has attempted to influence private wage and price decisions to moderate inflation; empirical analysis will never "prove" the success or failure of such efforts because it is impossible to determine what would have happened without controls. However, it is clear that wage and price pressures have sharply escalated. During the first quarter of 1974 the implicit GNP price deflator increased at a seasonally adjusted annual rate of 11.5 percent; the Consumer Price Index rose 12.2 percent; wholesale prices jumped 28.8 percent; and compensation per man-hour in the private nonfarm sector increased 6.8 percent. The controls program has clearly been unable to contain the wage and price pressures created by the convergence of strong demand forces and serious supply constraints. On April 30, 1974, the statutory authority for the control program expired. The entire experience should now be evaluated for use in shaping future economic policies.

THE BACKGROUND OF CONTROLS

The annual rate of inflation in the United States has historically averaged about 2 percent. However, the pace began to accelerate after mid-1965 and reached an annual level of 6.1 percent in 1969 before

Reprinted, with permission, from The Canadian Business REVIEW 1, no. 3 (Summer 1974), published by the Conference Board in Ottawa, Canada.

TABLE 1.1

Regulations of the Controls Program, Phases II, III, and IV

Program General standards	Phase II (November 14, 1971, to January 11, 1973)	Phase III (January 11, 1973, to June 13, 1973)	Phase IV (August 12, 1973, to April 30, 1974)[a]
Prices	Percentage pass-through of allowable cost increases since last price increase, or from January 1, 1971, adjusted for productivity and volume offsets. Term limits pricing option available.	Self-administered standards of Phase II.	In most manufacturing and service industries, dollar-for-dollar pass-through of allowable cost increase since last fiscal quarter ending prior to January 11, 1973.
Profits margin limitations	Not to exceed margins of the best 2 of the 3 fiscal years before August 15, 1971. Not applicable if prices were not increased above base level, or if firms "purified" themselves.	Not to exceed margins of the best 2 fiscal years completed after August 15, 1968. No limitation if average price increase did not exceed 1.5 percent.	Same as Phase III, except that a firm that had not charged a price for any item above its base price, whichever was higher, was not subject to the limitation.
Wages	General standard of 5.5 percent. Exceptions made to correct gross inequities and for workers whose pay had increased less than 7 percent a year for the last 3 years. Workers earning less than $2.75 per hour were exempt. Increases in qualified fringe benefits permitted raising standard to 6.2 percent.	General Phase II standard, self-administered. Some special limitations. More flexibility with respect to specific cases. Workers earning less than $3.50 per hour were exempted after May 1.	Same self-administered standards as Phase III. Executive compensation limited.

2

Prenotification

Prices	Prenotification required for all firms with annual sales above $100 million, 30 days before implementation, approval required.	After May 2, 1973, prenotification required for all firms with sales above $250 million if price increases exceeded a weighted average of 1.5 percent.	Same as Phase II except that prenotified price increases could be implemented in 30 days unless CLC required otherwise.
Wages	For all increases of wages for units of 5,000 or more and for all increases above the standard regardless of the number of workers involved.	None	None
Reporting			
Prices	Quarterly for firms with sales over $50 million.	Quarterly for firms with sales over $250 million.	Quarterly for firms with sales over $50 million.
Wages	Pay adjustments below standard for units greater than 1,000 persons.	Pay adjustments for units greater than 5,000 persons.	Same as Phase III.
Special areas	Health, insurance, rent, construction, public utilities.	Health, food, public utilities, construction, petroleum.	Health, food, petroleum, construction, insurance, executive, and variable compensation.
Exemptions to price standards[b]	Raw agricultural commodities, import prices, export prices, firms with 60 or fewer employees.	Same as Phase II plus rents.	Same as Phase III plus manufactured feeds, cement, public utilities, lumber, copper, scrap, long-term coal contracts, automobiles, fertilizers, nonferrous metals except aluminum and copper, mobile homes, and semiconductors.

[a] It should be noted that extensive decontrol efforts reduced the coverage of controls for many industries during Phase IV.

[b] In some of these sectors wages were also exempted.

Source: Cost of Living Council (COLC).

3

receding to 5. 5 percent in 1970 and 3. 4 percent in both 1971 and 1972.
Consumer prices rose at a seasonally adjusted annual rate of 3. 8 percent in 1971, prior to the 90-day freeze. Price increases continued at
the relatively moderate rate of 2. 9 percent during the first half and 3. 9
percent during the second half of 1972, although inflation pressures
were accelerating by the end of the year and surged sharply upward in
1973.

It is interesting to speculate on the relative importance of the
laggard impact of monetary and fiscal policies of restraint, compared
to the role of the various control measures summarized in Table 1. 1.
Similar controversy persists over the share of current shortages and
investment distortions that should be attributed to the controls. However,
the most interesting questions concern the future. Can economic policy
decisions be improved? Do the moderating effects of controls justify the
market distortions? Is there a future role for wage and price controls?
The following discussion of their positive and negative effects provides
a background for attempting to answer these most difficult questions.

POSITIVE LESSONS

The controls program has emphasized several crucial requirements
for improving the management of the economy. Most of these lessons
must be applied whether or not controls are part of the package.

The federal government has a basic role in shaping the general
economic environment. Although federal spending comprises only 21
percent of the GNP in the United States, fiscal and monetary policies
influence the pace of the entire economy. Federal programs provide
the seed capital that attracts private investment and development of
markets. Tax policies influence the rate and type of consumption and
investment. Monetary policy determines the supply and cost of credit.
Experiences with controls over the last three years have made the
general public much more sensitive about the impact of government
decisions.

Government economic policies must be better coordinated, "to
promote maximum employment, production, and purchasing power."[1]
While the need is obvious, the achievement is difficult. Each government agency and program has a particular constituency and time frame
for priorities. Political considerations also affect legislative and administrative decisions. The result is too often a series of individual
programs that concentrate on specific problems but fail to focus on the
larger goals of growth, inflation, and employment. On the other hand,
the Cost of Living Council (COLC) demonstrated that it is possible to
operate an interagency program for considering economic issues in a
broader context.

Inflation control required basic supply actions. Perhaps the most significant benefit of the controls program was the emphasis placed on increasing supplies in many sectors. The interagency approach identified many specific policies that work against the general antiinflation effort. Examples of supply-increasing actions of the federal government during 1973 include termination of farm export subsidies; suspension of mandatory wheat acreage set-asides; sale of government reserves of commodities; review of marketing orders to encourage increased production of fruit and vegetables; permitting of livestock grazing on set-aside acreages; coordination of crop transportation efforts; increased import quotas (or suspension of imports) for dry milk, butter, cheese, sugar, and meat; voluntary export limitations and monitoring programs for scarce commodities; a new farm bill designed to stimulate production by adoption of a target price system to support farm income; a fuel allocation program for agriculture; the sale of minerals from federal stockpile; increased timber sales from national forests; and suspension of mandatory oil import quotas and tariffs subject to monitoring. None of these actions depended upon the existence of wage and price controls, but the COLC review process identified needed adjustments of this kind and provided necessary authority. The COLC also worked closely with the private sector to stimulate increased productivity and capital investment to reduce supply shortages. These actions represent only the beginning of what could be accomplished by a coordinated federal program to eliminate supply constraints.

Labor-management advisory committees can contribute to broad antiinflation programs. Various advisory committees played an important role in general, and specifically in the food, health care, and construction sectors, in which particularly difficult problems existed. The self-enforcement approach was dependent upon the cooperation of the private sector.

A general economic education program was accomplished. The COLC was relatively successful in increasing the public's general understanding of how the economy works. This was somewhat ironic because the goal was always one of moving away from controls back to free markets, and in effect the COLC attempted to communicate to the general public the importance of restoring efficient markets so that controls could be terminated.

Public hearings and press briefings helped open up the system. An unusual amount of public analysis and discussion resulted from the COLC's hearings and monitoring efforts. While the confidentiality of individual company communication was protected, a great deal was learned about the way the economic system actually works.

COLC controls demonstrated that it is possible to moderate pressures in some sectors of the economy. Despite the general surge of wages and prices throughout the economy during the period of controls, there were specific sectors in which pressures were alleviated. The best

example involves the improved construction cost situation. The COLC
arranged "agreements" with several major industries that required
moderation in wage and price demands in exchange for decontrol rulings.

The analysis of specific problems by the COLC emphasizes the
increasing impact of international economic development. The severe
inflation pressures experienced in 1973 were directly influenced by
three significant international situations: the worldwide demand for
food sharply increased U. S. exports; the convergence of rising demand
pressures around the world accentuated industrial commodity price pressures; and the realignment of exchange rates reduced the value of the
U.S. dollar. Domestic economic policies must become more sensitive
to international factors.

Officials have always been aware of these general relationships,
but nevertheless, the recent controls program demonstrated the need for
improving the analytical process. In more specific terms the experience
also indicates certain procedural requirements.

Wage and price controls must be consistent with monetary and
fiscal policies. During the early stages of the controls program the
lagged impact of restrictive monetary and fiscal policies established
in 1969 and 1970 moderated inflationary pressures. Once the effects
of domestic expansionary policies and the worldwide boom in demand
began to accelerate in 1972, it became impossible to restrain the wage
and price pressures. Unless economic policies are mutually reinforcing,
it is unrealistic to expect any controls program to function very long as
an effective restraint. Analysis of incomes policies in Europe and the
United States indicates that they are only effective in dealing with
short-term emergencies such as balance-of-payments distortions. The
typical experience is that the continued upward drift of prices rather
quickly destroys the support of workers when their "real" earnings
decline as inflation erodes the purchasing power of their controlled
wages. It is ironic that wage and price controls are usually called for
when inflationary pressures are already accelerating as a result of
previous monetary and fiscal policy decisions. It is naive to expect
income policies to offset the more powerful monetary and fiscal forces.

Controls must remain flexible and recognize changing sectoral and
international variables. In general the controls program depended upon
self-enforcement of the rules, with some monitoring activities performed
by the COLC. As the program evolved, flexible adjustments were made
to moderate the various distortions caused by interfering with the normal
allocation of resources. The COLC immediately exempted a sizeable
portion of the economy by excluding small businesses and regulated
industries. It also granted individual exceptions, lifted controls for
industries experiencing unusual shortages or investment difficulties,
and attempted to reduce barriers to increased productivity. Specific
flexibility was provided by allowing "term-limit" price increases whereby
companies could determine individual product prices as long as a

company-wide average was not exceeded, full "dollar-pass-through" for justified cost increases, and adjustments to the base time period used for calculating average profit margins. Price increases were permitted when "necessary for efficient allocation of resources or to maintain adequate levels of supply." The COLC held extensive public hearings and private sessions with business and labor leaders developing regulations and evaluating appeals.

It is possible to operate a controls program with a relatively small bureaucracy. The entire staff involved in the controls program numbered only about 1,500 people at the maximum. Agents of the Internal Revenue Service were used for collecting information and preparing studies. The vast bureaucracies developed in previous controls programs were fortunately avoided, and the phase-out procedures have been relatively easy.

The information system must be modified to provide effective monitoring control. The existing program for collecting and publishing economic and social statistics provides guidance for developing general policies, but it is inadequate for operating a controls program. Expanded information about individual industries and the sources and availability of commodities, and specific details about wage and salary agreements, will be required if wage and price controls are used again.

A specific program for returning to free markets must be developed. At the beginning of Phase IV it was decided that some industries should be exempted. Small businesses and rents were not controlled because of administrative difficulties. Lumber was exempted because there were no accumulated cost pressures that would force prices upward. Other industries, such as fertilizers and nonferrous metals, were subsequently decontrolled because of shortages and the buildup of export pressures resulting from foreign price increases. Several industries were decontrolled when they agreed to increase capital investment. The automobile sector was exempted when it agreed not to raise prices for 1974 model year cars beyond approved levels unless economic conditions changed drastically. These decontrol efforts increased the program's credibility by moving back to free markets and further moderated the buildup of pressures during the period of controls. This helped prevent a massive price bulge at the conclusion of the program.

NEGATIVE LESSONS

The 1971-74 U.S. experience with controls reaffirms the earlier lesson that wage and price restrictions cannot divert market forces for very long. In addition, several specific disadvantages of relying on controls should be noted.

The normal allocation of resources is distorted by controls. Free markets respond to supply and demand pressures by adjusting prices, which calibrate the value of goods and services under conditions of constant change. Controlled economies restrict output and contribute to shortages because transaction prices may not accurately reflect accumulated costs. The sharp increase in exports in 1973 was partly attributable to holding U. S. prices below the world market level. The production of food products was particularly disrupted as costs increased beyond allowable price adjustments.

Capital investment may be delayed or even curtailed. Price restrictions often evolve into profit controls as a means of providing an enforcement procedure. The uncertainties created about future profitability tend to reduce the attractiveness of some projects, particularly if the anticipated return is marginal. In a few cases the absolute reduction in profits restricts the cash flows needed for new investment. Since controls programs are supposed to be temporary, new investments may only be delayed. Nevertheless, the loss of production capacity is disadvantageous because increasing output is usually the most effective antiinflation action. The impact of controls in the covered sectors also distorts demand by shifting investment into uncontrolled industries.

The general public builds up the false expectation that controls will correct fundamental supply and demand problems without monetary and fiscal measures. Public opinion polls suggest that a sizeable majority continues to believe that governments can manipulate wages and prices by decree. When market forces fail to respond, the resulting criticism is rarely directed at the basic limitations of controls. Instead the government officials responsible for the program are maligned. In some unfortunate situations, controls are used as a smoke screen to avoid the politically unpopular, but necessary, discipline of monetary and fiscal measures.

External events often swamp the temporary restraint provided by controls. The powerful impact of converging international demand and agricultural production problems combined to increase food and industrial commodity prices in 1973. The unexpected escalation of petroleum prices similarly increased energy prices. Three years of strong gains in output in the U. S. economy strained the labor force and plant and equipment resources. The increasing interdependence with the international economy also makes it difficult to avoid external pressures. It is unrealistic to expect controls designed for temporary periods to overcome such basic pressures.

Temporarily holding down specific wage and price gains may distort long-term relationships. Wage and price increases serve a very valuable resource allocation function. For example, energy price increases have contributed to necessary conservation efforts by discouraging consumption. Artificially constraining price changes may simply delay the adjustment, with the result that reinforcing pressures accumulate to push subsequent changes beyond what otherwise might have occurred.

Wage and price decisions anticipate future controls requirements by increasing such rates to the maximum level to avoid freezes. As the controls program evolved there was probably some "anticipatory" inflation created as companies established maximum list prices to protect against subsequent freezes; the 60-day freeze declared in June 1973 validated this concern. It is also possible that some of the arithmetic guidelines became a "floor" rather than a "ceiling" for wage and price increases.

The responsiveness of the private sector appears to diminish over time. The voluntary cooperation of the private sector was generally excellent throughout the entire period, but there was some erosion as distortions accumulated and uncertainties about the continuation of the program developed. The first 90-day freeze in August 1970 created widespread response, but the second 60-day freeze in June 1973 did not receive the same support.

The private sector is now very skeptical about the possible restoration of controls. Although the legislation authorizing wage and price controls expired April 30, 1974, and the COLC concluded its operations on June 30, many business and labor leaders fully anticipate that future political pressures created by public opinion support of controls will result in the restoration of some type of intervention. Price and wage decisions will continue to reflect this basic skepticism for some time.

SUMMARY

The debate over the efficacy of wage and price controls will undoubtedly continue, and various groups will continue to advocate their use in the future. Although conclusive evidence is unavailable, the historical experience in the United States and Europe indicates that controls are ineffective when fundamental market forces are adverse. Even temporary moderating benefits must be compared against the resulting distortions in the allocation of resources. To achieve lasting economic stability, more stable fiscal and monetary policies are required, to establish a favorable environment for the private markets to function. Specific efforts to stimulate productivity by removing structural and regulatory barriers to increased output also help reduce inflation pressures, but such efforts are not dependent upon the existence of a program of controls.

Wage and price controls are often popular with the general public because they demonstrate active government efforts to curtail unpopular inflation. However, political popularity should not justify economic programs that result in net disadvantages. The hard choices involving monetary and fiscal restraint cannot be avoided by turning to wage and price controls. Each experience with controls emphasizes the basic requirement that fiscal and monetary policies be consistent with other efforts to curtail inflation.

NOTE

1. U.S. Congress Joint Economic Committee, Employment Act of 1946, as amended, with related laws, 92nd cong., 1st. sess., April 1971, p. 1.

2

PRICE CONTROLS:
LESSONS FROM
RECENT EXPERIENCE
Jerry E. Pohlman

When the nation's first peacetime experiment with wage and price controls ended in April 1974, few expressions of regret were heard. Instead, the demise of controls occasioned discernible sighs of relief throughout the business as well as the labor community. Nor did consumers bemoan the event. Instead, their attitude was one of resigned indifference. Controls, from the consumer viewpoint, had not stopped inflation; therefore their removal was little cause for concern. In short, the euphoria that had accompanied the introduction of the New Economic Policy in August 1971 had, by the summer of 1974, been replaced by cynicism, indifference, and downright disgust.

It is useful to assess some of the lessons that can be drawn from this first fledgling U. S. peacetime experiment with an incomes policy. Phases I through IV are hardly likely to be the last of the nation's efforts to grapple with inflation through direct means. Inflationary pressures display few signs of receding, and no innovative economic policies to deal with the inflation-unemployment dilemma appear on the immediate horizon. Indeed, inflation and its wrenching social effects may well continue as one of the nation's most vexing economic problems throughout the 1970s. As a result, the largely discredited New Economic Policy is likely to be a forerunner of several additional "Phases" in the future. The extent of unemployment necessary to achieve price stability is both socially and politically unacceptable. At the same time, the American social fabric will not tolerate continuing seiges of double-digit inflation. Thus, in spite of their current unpopularity, it is highly likely that several forms of direct controls will be devised and implemented in the not-too-distant future. This being the case, it behooves us to consider some of the important lessons that can be derived from the recently ended controls of Phases I through IV.

CAN CONTROLS WORK ?

The costs involved in the operation of a price and wage control program are not insignificant. Compliance with their complex regulations imposes substantial costs upon business firms, while the administration of the program imposes costs upon taxpayers. In addition, there are the intangible, yet very real, costs of increased governmental intervention into the everyday affairs of workers, businessmen, and consumers. These expenses make sense only if they are outweighed by the benefits of the program; that is, if the controls work.

Roughly put, the test of the success of a controls program is whether or not prices are lower than they would have been in the absence of controls, other things being equal. The "other things being equal" is important, since if lower prices are only achieved by creation of a substantial number of market distortions, inefficiencies, and lost freedoms, the programs might well be considered unsuccessful.*

The relative success or failure of the Economic Stabilization Program of 1971-74 will long be the subject of study and debate. While it is currently fashionable to insist that price and wage controls have not worked and indeed that they cannot work, there is a considerable body of evidence that points in the other direction. [1] In my judgment, the evidence supports the contention that during Phase II prices rose 1.5 to 2 percent less than would have been the case in the absence of controls. In addition, given the expansionary monetary and fiscal policies that this allowed, unemployment was probably about 1 percent less than it would otherwise have been. † This is not to suggest that the program was entirely effective and without costs. This was hardly the case. It does suggest, however, that direct controls will remain an important consideration of any serious antiinflation policy of the future.

----

*Wage rates are not susceptible to the same test. Lower wages are not attractive alone, but only with respect to their effect on prices. With a given level of productivity improvement, lower wages imply lower prices. The "end" of the controls policy is reduced price inflation, not poorer workers.

†Lest these gains appear insignificant, it should be noted that a 1 percent increase in unemployment implies nearly 900,000 additional persons out of work and nearly $35 billion in foregone output.

THE LESSONS OF EXPERIENCE

If controls, as suggested above, have had a beneficial impact, why are they currently held in such universally low esteem? Businessmen, trade unionists, and consumers—to say nothing of professional economists—are less than enchanted with price and wage controls. The reasons for this are discussed on the following pages.

Lesson No. 1: Don't Expect Too Much

The economic policy inaugurated in August 1971 was intended to be a bold and dramatic move that would counter inflationary forces while stimulating the economy in an attempt to reduce unemployment. There can be little doubt that the Administration was successful in having its new policy viewed in those terms. The dramatic wage and price freeze raised hopes that, at last, the Administration was "doing something" to turn the economy around. However, this initial overselling of the policy did much to lead to the disillusionment that set in later when the controls failed to live up to expectations.

It is understandable that large segments of the public are disappointed with the perceived results of wage and price controls. The present disillusionment within the economics profession, however, is somewhat more difficult to understand. Wage and price controls can form only one parameter of a complex interaction of economic institutions and policies. This seemingly obvious fact is often overlooked by those who would cite the price increases during 1972 and 1973 as "proof" that the controls had no impact.

This reaction among professional observers seems somewhat strange. It is generally agreed that any one public policy can have only a marginal impact on the state of the economy. It is the total combination of policies, in conjunction with broad economic forces, that shapes the behavior of the economy over a given period of time. To believe otherwise is to believe that the controls program had complete power over wage and price movements and could be judged accordingly. Such, of course, was neither the design nor the intent of the Economic Stabilization Program. Nor will it, one hopes, be the intent of future control programs.

If an economy as large, vibrant, and diversified as that of the United States ever becomes completely susceptible to one particular policy lever, we will have moved light years away from anything resembling a competitive, individualistic environment. To assert that a policy is only marginally effective, however, is not to deprecate its importance. This is the nature of most policy movements, and one might convincingly argue that we are all better off (although many times highly frustrated) because of it.

Monetary and fiscal policies provide a case in point. At any given time, a directional change in these policies will have only a marginal impact; that is, their effect on the direction of the economy will be limited. The failure of restrictive monetary and fiscal policies to stem the rising tide of inflation in 1970 and 1971 demonstrates just how marginal these policies can be. To conclude from this that these policy tools are unimportant or ineffective, however, would clearly be fallacious.

The fact that the results of this first peacetime attempt at wage and price controls had only a limited impact (and some quite undesirable side effects) certainly is not convincing evidence of the inappropriateness of this policy under the proper circumstances.

Lesson No. 2: The Environment of the Program is Crucial

As with any public policy, one would expect price controls to be increasingly successful the more they operate in conjunction with other policies and economic forces. This was hardly the case during 1973 when the program began to break down. First, monetary and fiscal policy had become extremely expansionary during 1972 in an attempt to bring the economy out of the planned recession of 1971 before election time. For example, the nation's money supply (M_1) rose at an annual rate of 8.2 percent during 1972, compared with an annual pace of 6.4 percent from 1970 through 1971. Similarly, deficit spending rose from a level of $12 billion in 1970 (after an actual surplus in 1969) to $22 billion in 1971 and another $17.5 billion in 1972, reaching an annual pace of $25.6 billion in the fourth quarter of that year. Even many economists who welcomed this expansion as a means of cutting into the high levels of unemployment were alarmed at the speed of the monetary and fiscal reversal. The result was a buildup of inflationary pressures.

At the same time, and in contrast to nearly all previous periods, the entire Western World was experiencing a simultaneous economic upturn. This had the effect of placing many raw materials under extremely severe demand-pull pressures and, when output was unable to respond sufficiently because of capacity bottlenecks, the result was as inevitable as it was dramatic: widespread shortages combined with soaring prices.

The two official devaluations of the dollar, in August 1971 and January 1973, combined with the later unofficial devaluation resulting from floating exchange rates, added further momentum to domestic price movements. Imports became more expensive while exports became highly attractive to foreign buyers, thereby exacerbating already severe commodity shortages in the United States.

Finally, worldwide declines in agricultural production in 1972, combined with the Administration's shortsighted approval of the now infamous Russian wheat deal, led to skyrocketing food prices.

This, then, was the prevailing economic environment when the controls program was suddenly switched to the "self-administered" Phase III in January 1973. Only the most optimistic and naive observer would expect a largely voluntary incomes policy to be able to restrain the onslaught of price increases under these pressures. The lesson is clear: an incomes policy cannot be expected to single-handedly contain massive price pressures from other sources. Controls can have a useful, but marginal, impact. They cannot become a substitute for well-formulated actions in such critical areas as monetary and fiscal policy, agricultural policy, international trade policy, and antitrust policy.

Lesson No. 3: The Direction of Controls is Important

The level of the current discussions concerning an incomes policy would lead one to assume that there is one form of wage and price controls and one form only, that controls are controls are controls. Current discussions center largely on whether price and wage controls can be effective. While this is certainly a relevant and important concern, one rarely encounters discussion of what does or does not constitute an effective control program. To the extent that public policy will continue to implement different control policies in the future, this latter question is highly significant and of immediate concern.

The question of "having" an incomes policy is no more sufficient than the question of "having" a monetary policy. Monetary policy can be good or bad depending upon one's viewpoint and right or wrong depending upon economic circumstances. Observers who disagree with the direction of monetary policy, however, seldom argue that the policy has no impact. Instead, they argue that a given policy is inappropriate under the circumstances. Similar considerations, of course, apply to fiscal policy.

The fact of "having" an incomes policy does not, by itself, insure that the policy will be successful. The policy may be inappropriate for the economic conditions in which it is operating; it may be an ill-designed policy; as mentioned above, it may be in sharp variance with other very powerful forces operating within the economy.

While there is a sizeable body of economic literature dealing with the unemployment-inflation "trade-off," there is a paucity of analysis concerned with the internal mechanisms of various incomes policies. This is understandable, since only recently did we experience our first peacetime use of such a policy. Still, the unmistakable impression given is that controls are controls, period. Little serious thought is given to alternative degrees of coverage, various control mechanisms and their differing impact, or other "internal" considerations; yet the differences in these mechanisms can greatly alter the impact of the program both directly on price movements and indirectly on the various secondary side effects of the program.

For example, it is frequently argued that price controls were responsible for the many shortages that began to occur in late 1973 and 1974.
While controls undoubtedly received undue blame for these shortages,
there can be little doubt that they were a contributing factor. Future
controls programs should concern themselves more with the allocative
impact they have on the economy and be more sensitive to pressure
points as they develop. In this sense, the "rules" of Phases II, III,
and IV were representative of a first attempt to deal with an exceedingly
complex problem. There can be little doubt that this policy tool needs
refinement and increased sophistication.

The development of more sophisticated control mechanisms that
will enhance the effectiveness of controls while minimizing undesirable
side effects will come about as the inevitability of future controls programs becomes more apparent. A part of the reluctance to deal more
effectively with these "micro" policies undoubtedly stems from the fact
that delving directly into the market place is a much more messy business than pulling and pushing broad policy levers of great monetary
and fiscal magnitude. The failure of these traditional policies to deal
effectively with the unemployment-inflation dilemma, however, insures
that direct measures will continue to be applied. Increasing the attention paid to the internal mechanism of these measures will increase
their future effectiveness. Hopefully, we can look forward to increased
discussion of the appropriateness of various types of incomes policies
along with the continuing discussion concerning the efficacy of controls in general.

Lesson No. 4: The Nature of the Controls is Critical

The decision was made shortly after the inception of the wage and
price control program in 1971 that, in order to gain widespread public
acceptance, controls would have to apply equally to all sectors of the
economy. Politically, this may have been important; economically, the
wisdom of such a policy is dubious, to say the least.

The fallacy lies in assuming a homogeneity of the economy that
simply does not exist. Some sectors of the economy are susceptible
to external regulation while others are not. Given the complexity of
the U.S. economy, attempts to explain wage and price movement in all
sectors with one economic model are doomed to failure. A controls
program that, in effect, makes this assumption is fated for a similar
ending.

All sorts of anomalies and distortions erupt because the impact
of the same policy is felt much differently in different sectors of the
economy. Put another way, in order to achieve a similar impact on
different sectors of the economy, differing policy tools must be constructed. This approach was attempted during the latter months of the
economic stabilization program (Phase IV), but by then the game was

largely over and the panicky, last-ditch attempt at an industry-by-industry approach had no real chance to be effective.

The point is not <u>whether</u> a sector of the economy will be controlled, but <u>how</u> it will be controlled. Some segments of the economy are tightly "controlled" by competition, while others, on the oligopolistic and monopolistic end of the spectrum, are much more isolated from competitive forces. External control through an incomes policy makes sense, and can work, only in those sectors of the economy that are not sufficiently controlled by competition.

The competitive areas of the economy are still responsive to the conventional economic tools of monetary and fiscal policy, and they expand and contract in the expected directions. This is not true of the oligopolistic power sectors, where unintended consequences often follow the application of restrictive policies. With a downturn in demand resulting from a spending contraction, the oligopolistic sectors adjust by lowering output instead of prices. The result is increased unemployment rather than falling or stable prices. Indeed, to the extent that unit costs increase with a decrease in output (because of a smaller base over which to spread fixed costs), firms in these sectors may increase prices even further in an attempt to maintain profits. Thus, monetary and fiscal controls in oligopolistic sectors fail to have their intended effect, and an alternative form of control is called for. The control needed is of a more direct type that will not result in decreased output and increased unemployment. It is here that the case for a well-formulated incomes policy is the strongest.

In sectors of the economy that approach the competitive model, external price controls can do little good but much harm. By setting prices below equilibrium levels, controls create serious distortions, shortages, and bottlenecks while doing little to alleviate price pressures. In the less competitive sectors of the economy, however, controls can force a "solution" that is closer to the competitive norm than would be the case in their absence. By removing price increases as a means of increasing profits or adjusting to a drop in demand, controls can promote the achievement of simultaneously reduced inflation and increased employment. In oligopolistic markets the arguments against controls are much less persuasive, since distortions already exist as a result of the market power of business and labor.

The placement of mandatory controls on virtually all sectors of the economy coincided with worldwide food shortages during Phases III and IV. The result was a shortfall of supply, upward pressure on prices, and controls biting the hardest in one of the most competitive sectors of the economy, namely agriculture. The effect quickly illustrated what happens when controls are clamped fairly tightly onto a competitive situation suffering from demand-pull inflationary pressures. Then, from the resulting and quite predictable market shortages, distortions, and evasions it was promptly concluded by economists, as well as the general public, that all controls were indeed inefficient and ineffective.

Most observers who are sympathetic toward the imposition of an incomes policy agree that such policies can be the most effective during periods of cost-push inflation centered in oligopolistic sectors of the economy. The fact that controls were relatively ineffective in restraining prices in competitive sectors of the market during a period of extreme demand-pull pressures hardly negates their appropriateness in the former circumstances. With the current demise in public and professional support for wage and price controls, such distinctions are seldom made.

In the future, increased attention must be given to formulating a control program that can be effective in some sectors of the economy while at the same time coordinating this policy with other policy tools in the more competitive sectors. This will require a more sophisticated and thought-out approach to economic stabilization than we have seen so far. The required effort, however, is well matched by the seriousness of the problem with which it is dealing.

Lesson No. 5: The Administration of Controls is Important

During the Economic Stabilization Program, it was a source of pride among many government administrators that the controls were run by a relatively small group of persons. In light of subsequent experiences, this policy is open to serious question. The effect of the small staff, coupled with broad coverage, was quite understandable and predictable: an ineffective job.

A more logical approach would be to determine those sectors of the economy in which controls could be of use and then attempt to determine the number of persons it would take to run the program in an equitable and effective manner. These costs could then be compared with the estimated benefits of the undertaking. If the former exceeded the latter, the idea should be scrapped; if not, the program could proceed.

The shortage of staff and the breadth of coverage led to another major shortcoming of the Economic Stabilization Program, which was the severe lack of responsiveness that the program, especially in its later stages, was able to provide to business, labor, and consumer groups. In my judgment it was this lack of responsiveness from public officials to their constituency regarding legitimate questions and problems that led, even more than the impact of the regulations themselves, to the program's mounting disfavor with the public during the latter half of 1973 and early 1974. It was during this time that the worldwide pressures were rapidly mounting, and the inequities built into a system of universal controls began to display themselves. More than ever, the program needed to be responsive to these pressures. The clear need was to move swiftly and effectively to provide relief where it was warranted and control where it was needed. Unfortunately, the program demonstrated no such responsiveness. Instead, the prevailing attitude was one of "we'll show them how tough controls can be," along with indifferent delays and postponements of individual and collective requests for action.

At the top levels of government there was a conscious desire to demonstrate that controls could not work. To make the point, all that was needed was an unresponsive attitude to the developing problems. In this sense the "true" policy—to demonstrate the inequities and distortions a controls program could lead to—was highly successful.

At the staff level there was a desire on the part of some to show how "tough" they could be toward various business interests. The impact on the economy became secondary to the display of power on the part of various staff controllers. At the same time there was a growing feeling of indifference on the part of many which, combined with inadequate staffing, led to unconscionable delays in responding to individual price increase and exceptions requests. There is little wonder that business and labor leaders, in dealing with an unresponsive and increasingly capricious bureaucracy, became disenchanted with the entire apparatus.

The business and labor communities, I believe, recognized the inflationary course that the economy had embarked upon in the late 1960s. In addition, these groups were willing to sacrifice (so long as others also sacrificed) in order to make the Economic Stabilization Program work. At the same time, business and labor expected the government, in return for their cooperation and support, to be responsive to the real problems that the program caused. In this they were sorely disappointed. Without the staff it needed to be responsive, the Cost of Living Council swiftly and seriously eroded business, labor, and consumer confidence to a point at which voluntary compliance was exceedingly difficult to achieve; and voluntary cooperation, even though the program was made mandatory in Phase IV after the Phase III experiment with "self-administered" guidelines, was extremely crucial.

Coinciding with the lack of personnel and responsiveness by stabilization officials was the seeming lack of concern by the Administration for either the purpose of the program or its unintended side effects. Consumers sensed that the Administration was less than serious in its supposed "war on inflation"; businessmen sensed a lack of concern with legitimate problems that arose from the controls; and labor felt that the entire deck was stacked against it. This is hardly an environment in which one could expect public confidence to flourish.

The Administration promptly implanted feelings of doubt during the first months of Phases III and IV by making all sorts of public pronouncements about how soon controls would be lifted—controls which, they hinted, could not be expected to work anyway. Everyone was made well aware of the Administration's acute distaste for the policy it was pursuing. One could hardly expect a monetary policy headed by persons who believed that any monetary policy could do no good, and furthermore that the Federal Reserve should be dismantled, to be a shining

success. It does not even take the advantages of hindsight to see why
the public displayed less than overwhelming enthusiasm for a policy
in which the Administration itself showed a visible lack of confidence
and, indeed, outright disdain.

Lesson No. 6: Voluntary Controls are Insufficient

While a high degree of voluntary cooperation is necessary for any
governmental program to succeed, it can hardly be doubted that a
successful incomes policy must be mandatory rather than voluntary in
nature. During a period of voluntary or "self-administered" guidelines,
those businessmen and unions that gain the most are those that simply
ignore the rules. This, in turn, quickly erodes the degree of cooperation forthcoming from other groups.

This was amply demonstrated during the Phase III "self-administered"
period of the Economic Stabilization Program. Those businessmen who
rushed the fastest to increase prices in anticipation of another price
freeze were rewarded with higher base prices when the freeze—which
their actions helped to bring about—materialized. At the same time,
those who voluntarily cooperated with the program and followed the
guidelines were punished by having low base prices. Few of these
latter businessmen will make the same mistake the next time around.

During a period of inflation, it is in the interests of each individual
businessman and employee to raise his prices and wages as much as
he possibly can. To do so is only to be concerned with one's welfare
during a period of high uncertainty. To do otherwise is to fall increasingly behind without having any appreciable or discernible impact on
the rate of inflation. In short, inflation cannot be fought by individuals
acting alone, and those who try, quickly end up looking and feeling as
if the had "been had."

It is only through a public policy that this fallacy of composition
can be broken. If compliance with the program can be made widespread,
as it can only with a mandatory program, the individual actions of
thousands of decision-makers can be directed toward the public (and
individual) benefit and the upward spiral of prices, wages, and costs
endlessly chasing each other can be broken.

THE INEVITABILITY OF CONTROLS

Regardless of the current mood concerning incomes policies, it is
likely that any respite from direct government intervention in wage and
price determination will be short-lived. Public demands combined with
economic forces conspire to make such actions inevitable.

The public will not tolerate a sustained high rate of unemployment,
and certainly it will not tolerate levels of unemployment anywhere near

those that would be necessary for price stability. The rates of inflation experienced in 1974 are clearly intolerable. Already social unrest and reaction to this degree of inflation are becoming ominous. Such conditions will not be accepted, and in the final analysis the public will turn to nearly any promise of stability for relief from inflationary turmoil. If moderate solutions cannot be found, radical ones will be.

The truth of the matter is that conventional monetary and fiscal policies are not able, and cannot be counted upon, to deal effectively with the major societal problem. Thus it will again be necessary to deal with the unemployment-inflation dilemma through direct means. Hopefully, serious attention will begin to be focused on the means by which this can be done so that our next experiment with wage and price controls can be more systematic, effective, and equitable than our last one. While Phases I through IV accomplished much toward our understanding of economic stabilization efforts, by their being, as they were, hesitant and fledgling initial steps, many errors of commission as well as omission were made. Hopefully these errors, along with the many successes of the program, will provide useful lessons for the future.

NOTE

1. See, for example, Robert J. Gordon, "Wage-Price Controls and the Shifting Phillips Curve," Brookings Papers on Economic Activity no. 2, (1972): 385-430. Barry Bosworth, "Phase II: The U. S. Experiment with an Incomes Policy," Brookings Papers on Economic Activity, no. 2, (1972): 343-383. Robert F. Lanzilotti and Blaine Roberts, "The Legacy of Phase II Price Controls" American Economic Review, 64, no. 2, (May 1974): 82-87.

CHAPTER

3

**WAGE-PRICE CONTROLS IN
ADMINISTRATIVE AND
POLITICAL PERSPECTIVE:
THE CASE OF THE PRICE
COMMISSION DURING PHASE II**
A. Bradley Askin

Although employed in a number of developed Western nations for antiinflationary purposes during the postwar era, mandatory incomes policies (especially direct wage and price controls) were consistently rejected in the United States prior to 1971 as improper interferences with the market mechanism. Controls were imposed as emergency measures in both World War II and the Korean conflict, but were never instituted on a systematic basis in peacetime.* Incomes policies could suppress inflation in the short run, the overwhelming majority of U. S. economists and policy makers said, but caused distortions and eventually broke down in the long run when demand pressures mounted. [1]

Things changed dramatically on August 15, 1971, when for the first time in its peacetime history the United States entered the worldwide incomes-policy derby. Plagued by a stubborn inflation that had accelerated over several years despite a succession of "game plans" and pressed by calls for action emanating from all sides, President Nixon announced a 90-day freeze on all wages and prices in an abrupt reversal of earlier policies followed by his Administration. [2] Billed as merely a crucial, first-stage element in a "New Economic Policy," the freeze was to be superseded by Phases II and III, returning the economy to its normal, decontrolled state in a short, if indefinite, amount of time after inflation had been broken. [3]

---

*Specific instances of mandatory controls, such as those on interest rates, have been in existence for some time. However, the wage-price guideposts of the 1960s and the "jaw-boning" that superseded them were voluntary programs without force of law or enforcement provisions. Presidents Kennedy and Johnson applied them in selected industries on an ad hoc basis through the force of moral suasion and the power of their office.

Initially, controls were hailed as the proper course, an idea for which the day had come, and even skeptics adopted a wait-and-see attitude for the most part; yet by the time they were finally removed nearly three years later at the end of June 1974, the controls were almost universally categorized a failure, an idea for which the day had passed.* Careful examination of the evidence supports neither of these extreme views. For at least their first 14 months the controls were associated with a reduced rate of inflation, even though doomed to have diminishing impact over time owing to operating regulations that encouraged and institutionalized cost-push inflation.[4]

The Nixon controls program cannot be properly assessed solely on the basis of formal economic analysis. To fully understand and properly evaluate the recent controls interlude, such economic analysis must be placed in administrative and political context. This chapter seeks to provide the needed perspective on Price Commission operations during Phase II. Turning away from a purely technical analysis of the Price Commission operating regulations and the economic events associated with them, it explores the manner in which certain features of the Price Commission and its Phase II environment affected the development and implementation of commission policies.

Sections II and III of the paper make two important points. First, the Price Commission focused too much on noneconomic considerations in setting policy, with the result that it frequently adopted policies inappropriate for curbing inflation. Second, the Nixon Administration failed to provide the commission with the resources and moral support needed to effectively fight inflation. In the fourth section of this chapter, alternative explanations for the points made in the second and third sections are briefly explored. Prescriptions for future controls efforts and new government programs in general are then presented in the final section.

ADMINISTRATORS AS POLICY MAKERS:
THE FLAWED PRICE COMMISSION EFFORT

From inception the Price Commission was handicapped by its internal organizational makeup and its decision structure. Viable economic

---

*Although organized labor expressed reservations about the imposition of controls, its representatives agreed to serve on the Pay Board after receiving assurances that the decisions of that body would not be reversed by the Nixon Administration. Four of the five labor representatives blasted, and resigned from, the Pay Board, only after they were outvoted by its business and public members in several key cases.

policy can be formulated only when thorough and competent economic analysis is conducted. At the Price Commission, where the essential mission called for setting and implementing economic policy, the requisite economic analysis was often relegated to the background if not missing or ignored.

Economists were in short supply at the Price Commission. Most members of the staff had backgrounds in accounting, law, or management. Although the size of the staff quickly expanded to 700 positions, probably no more than 15 to 20 professional economists were ever employed by the commission at any time.* For much of Phase II, particularly at the beginning when the policy development need was greatest, even fewer economists were present.

The shortage of economists was most notable in the upper echelons of the commission staff. The large majority of economists worked in the Office of Price Policy; two or three acted as in-house consultants in the Office of Program Operations; and one served on the staff of the commission chairman for the second half of Phase II.† Only three economists held staff positions with significant policy-setting duties or direct access to the top people with that power, two of them in the Office of Price Policy. None of the three had unfettered contact with the commissioners.

----

*Estimating the number of legitimate economists at the Price Commission is more difficult than it might appear. Civil Service records would undoubtedly show that a large number of economists worked at the Price Commission, but only 24 credit hours in college economics, far fewer hours than are needed for even a B.A. in economics, are required to qualify as an economist before the Civil Service Commission. Robert Lanzillotti, one of the former Price Commissioners who is an economist, has placed the number of academic economists ever on the commission staff at 8 and the total number of economists on it at between 20 and 25. In my view, 15 is a realistic estimate of the maximum number of economists employed by the Commission at any time and 20 an upper bound.

†The Office of Price Policy was charged with interpreting the data and statistical reports released by other government agencies; identifying and commenting on policy options; monitoring the performance of the Price Commission in slowing inflation; and performing special studies. Most of the time it reacted to events, operating on a very short turnaround time: there was seldom opportunity to do long-run or in-depth analyses. The Office of Program Operations was responsible for the day-to-day operations of the commission in reviewing firm reports and approving or denying their requests for permission to raise prices.

Since economists were scarce, the bulk of policy setting and decision making was forced on individuals with little training in advanced
economics or experience in analyzing the complex forces at work in a
trillion-dollar economy. The commission exacerbated the situation by
adopting a centralized decision process that funneled policy issues up
the hierarchy by means of *e* iterative series of reviews at successively
higher levels of the staff. This iteration of reviews effectively limited the
the direct inputs of economists to lower levels of the organization and
at the same time elevated nearly all decisions to higher levels where
economists had little voice. As a consequence, as most policy issues
progressed up the Price Commission chain of command toward final
resolution, less attention was focused on economic considerations and
more on administrative concerns such as ease of enforcement and noninterference with business. *

The devaluation economic analysis in the policy-setting process
reached its peak, and to a considerable degree originated, with the
Price Commissioners. Five of the seven commissioners—including the
chairman, C. Jackson Grayson, a business school dean with a doctorate
in business administration and prior experience as a FBI agent, news-
paperman, and cost accountant, who headed both the commission and
its staff—were noneconomists without special expertise in inflation. †
As a group, the commissioners were undoubtedly less attuned to the
complex economic aspects of price controls or competent to deal with
them than the commission staff. Both in word and deed they displayed
as much concern with the President's caveats against creating another

---

*The shift in emphasis reflected both the shortage of economists
and their separation from power and the background of higher-level
Price Commission staffers and their natural tendency to focus on
those factors they could handle most competently. For most policy
issues, the Office of Price Policy was asked early in the policy-
setting process to identify and briefly evaluate the options open to
the Price Commission. Sometimes the analyst responsible for the
initial study was then asked to present his views at later stages of
the review process. This invitation was not automatic, however, and
often meant little owing to the fact that the analyses requested of,
and produced by, the Office of Price Policy tended to be superficial.

†When one of the two economists appointed to the commission
resigned to join the Council of Economic Advisors, she was replaced
by another economist. The chairman was delegated day-to-day operating authority by the full commission because the other commissioners
only served part-time.

federal bureaucracy or interfering unduly with normal business practice
as with keeping prices down.*

It would be an error to argue that the administrative considerations
focused on by the Price Commission in setting policy were irrelevant or
unimportant; however, the commission overemphasized these factors
to the exclusion of economic analysis. It could have slowed the rate
of inflation during Phase II more effectively by paying greater attention
to economic analysis when evaluating and choosing among alternative
policies. A review of three policy decisions made by the commission
illustrates this point.

At the start of Phase II, firms seeking to cost-justify price increases
to the Price Commission were instructed to calculate by their regular
accounting procedures the extent to which productivity gains had offset
cost increases. The rationale for allowing firms to use their regular
methods in computing the offset was to minimize for the firms the cost
and administrative burden of modifying accounting practices or keeping
extra records just for the Price Commission. However, owing to the
fact that most firms had not kept records on productivity and thus had
no regular accounting procedures for doing so, the effect was to allow
firms to manipulate and understate their true productivity gains and
obtain approval for larger price increases than were justified through
the judicious choice of productivity-offset accounting procedures. The
Price Commission instituted a new, tougher standard assigning to all
firms the average productivity gains reported for their industries by
the Bureau of Labor Statistics only when a staff study almost midway
through Phase II documented the statistical impossibility that virtually
all firms were reporting productivity gains less than those averages.

Throughout Phase II, firms were permitted to maintain their cus-
tomary profit margins, or mark-ups of prices over unit costs, when
raising prices to compensate for cost increases. At the urging of
both inside and outside economists, the Price Commission on several
occasions considered replacing this policy with a more stringent one
that would have allowed only a dollar-for-dollar pass-through of

---

*When testifying before Congress for instance, chairman Grayson
invariably noted that the Price Commission had multiple goals including
noninterference with recovery and holding down the bureaucracy. See
U.S. Congress Joint Economic Committee, Hearings on Review of Phase
II of the New Economic Program, April 14, 18-31, 24, 1972, 92nd cong.,
2nd sess., (Washington, D.C.: U.S. Government Printing Office, 1972),
pp. 91-93; U.S. Senate Committee on Banking, Housing and Urban
Affairs, Hearings on Economic Stabilization Legislation—1973, January
29-31, February 1, 5-7, 1973, 93rd cong., 1st sess. (Washington, D.C:
U.S. Government Printing Office, 1974), pp. 101-103.

increased costs. Acknowledging its deleterious long-run impingement
on the return to capital, proponents of the change nevertheless urged
it for the short run during Phase II in order to give firms more incentive
to hold costs down and to prevent inflation from cumulating as price
increases worked their way through the economy.* Each time it recon-
sidered the issue, however, the Price Commission reaffirmed its original policy on the unwarranted grounds of not interfering with the rules
of thumb typically followed by businesses in setting their markup
margins.†

---

*Under the constant markup policy, profitable firms with prices
more than covering unit costs could increase their profits per unit of
output by letting costs go up and then raising prices the same percentage that costs had increased. Doing this could raise total profits in
certain circumstances. The dollar-for-dollar pass-through policy would
have eliminated the incentive to let costs rise, since under it firms
would have been able to raise prices only enough to offset their cost
increases and keep profits per unit of output constant. Under the constant mark up policy a rise in the cost of one item could lead to a
larger increase in its price and then still a larger increase in the price
of a second item made from the first one. Under the dollar-for-dollar
pass-through policy, an increase in the unit cost for one item could
never raise its price by more than the initial unit cost increase nor lead
to a larger increase in the price of another item made from the first one.

†The impact of the proposed change on markup rules of thumb would
have been trivial. Denote price by P, unit costs by C, profit per unit
of output by R, and the markup rate by M. Then $P = C + R$ and $P = C(1
+ M)$. M was fixed under the constant markup policy, so that firms
could simply substitute a new value of C into the second equation and
recalculate P after an increase in unit costs. R would have been fixed
instead of M under the proposed dollar-for-dollar pass-through policy,
forcing firms either to use the first equation when unit costs rose or to
compute a new value for M in the second equation. If switching from
the second equation to the first one would have imposed too big a
burden on firms, recomputing M and using the second equation would
have required nothing more than multiplying the old value of M by the
ratio of the old unit cost to the new unit costs. Substituting in the two
equations above gives

$$M = \frac{R}{C}$$

Remembering that the proposed dollar-for-dollar pass-through policy
would have fixed R, simple algebra gives

Early in Phase II, when all firms were required to justify price increases on an item-by-item basis by documenting cost increases for each product, it became clear that both the dollar and manpower costs of compliance would be astronomical for large conglomerates, which produce literally thousands of products, and that the Price Commission would be unable to effectively monitor all submissions. As a response to this problem the Price Commission introduced term-limit pricing (TLP) agreements. TLP firms were allowed to cost-justify their price increases on a company-wide, instead of product-by-product, basis and were given flexibility about which specific prices they raised. In return they agreed not to raise the weighted average of all their prices by more than the cost-justified percentage and not to raise individual prices by more than certain maximum percentages determined through negotiation with the Price Commission.

In the words of one Price Commissioner, "the rationale for the TLP policy was administrative convenience rather than economic logic."[5] Had the Price Commission carried this to its logical conclusion and simply abolished controls, the results might not have been much different for TLP firms than those actually achieved. Implemented on the basis of a blueprint prepared primarily by Arthur Anderson and Company accountants working at the Price Commission under a consulting contract, TLP agreements proved far less effective in restraining inflation than the market mechanism they were supposed to supplement. TLP gave firms complete freedom to use cost increases that occurred in competitive markets and industries as justification for price increases in markets and industries where they had monopoly power, whether or not cost increases arose in the latter markets and industries. Few TLP firms found they could raise their prices on average as much as their TLP agreements allowed them to, so that signing TLP agreements cost them little.*

$$M_{new} = \left(M_{old}\right)\left(\frac{C_{old}}{C_{new}}\right)$$

as the markup that would be appropriate after an increase in unit costs. To argue that firms would have had to make major adjustments in their markup rules of thumb is nonsense.

*One internal Price Commission study never made public showed that on the average prices actually charged by all TLP firms had fallen even though the firms had been granted authority to raise prices by approximately 2 percent. This finding did not come as a surprise, for most TLP firms had experienced declining prices for several years. Effective antiinflationary rules would have required TLP firms to lower their prices even faster than they did in Phase II. This could have been

THE LACK OF NIXON ADMINISTRATION SUPPORT
FOR THE PRICE COMMISSION

Billed as autonomous, the Price Commission was actually subject to significant external control by the Nixon Administration. First, it was forced to work within the cost-justification and profit-margin limitation framework developed for Phase II price controls by Nixon Administration personnel during the 90-day freeze. Second, the commission had no permanent staff or appropriation of its own as part of the Cost of Living Council in the Executive Office of the President and had to rely on the Administration for resources. Third, there were overlaps of authority with the Cost of Living Council that were never fully resolved. Fourth, its lack of meaningful enforcement machinery or power meant the commission could derive credibility only from public acceptance as fostered or deterred by the moral support and leadership of the Administration. Hindered by its own inattention to economic analysis, the Price Commission consistently saw its effectiveness in fighting inflation further and far more severely reduced by the external operations of the Nixon Administration.

According to Nixon Administration spokesmen, the Phase II cost-justification and profit-margin limitation framework was specifically designed to halt the cost-push inflation at work when controls were imposed. Instead it institutionalized cost-push inflation by exerting minimal downward pressure on costs and allowing firms to raise prices only when costs rose. Only in late 1972 when the profit-margin limitation, originally intended to be of secondary importance, began to bite in response to rising aggregate demand did the Phase II regulations begin to prove effective, and shortly thereafter the Price Commission and Phase II were discontinued on the Catch-22 argument that they were no longer appropriate given a shift from cost-push to demand-pull inflation. *

---

done by denying them the power to cost-justify and offset price increases in monopolistic markets with cost increases and price declines, respectively, in competitive markets. A more sympathetic interpretation of the TLP policy is given in Mary T. Hamilton, "Price Controls in 1973: Strategies and Problems," American Economic Review 64, no. 2 (May 1974): 100-102.

*The Price Commission did exert some downward pressure on costs by letting firms cost-justifying price increases use only the first 5.5 percent of wage increases, by disallowing certain types of discretionary overhead cost increases, and during the second half of Phase II by requiring firms to use productivity figures obtained from the Bureau of Labor Statistics. Firms intent on cost-justifying price increases could

Lanzillotti and Roberts have estimated that in combination the 90-day freeze and Phase II yielded to the economy as a whole, dollar benefits between 7 and 26 times as large as the dollar costs they imposed on society. [6] This analysis, even though quite sensitive to the assumptions underlying it, suggests that the Nixon Administration could have afforded to allot substantial resources to its controls program even under the strictest of criteria. Yet the Administration limited the Price Commission to well under 1,000 of its own full-time employees and 3,000 Internal Revenue Service employees assigned to enforcement activities part time, whereas more than 60,000 paid employees and 300,000 unpaid volunteers had been required by the Office of Price Administration (OPA) during World War II to control an economy less than half as large in real terms. Economists were in short supply at the Price Commission, not only because it did not fully appreciate the need for them, but also because it faced stiff hiring constraints.

Recent econometric studies indicate that price expectations have played a major role in feeding inflation since the late 1960s. [7] Given the fundamental weakness of its framework and operating regulations, the only way the Price Commission could realistically hope to do more than delay inflation in a snarl of bureaucratic red tape was to create a stabilization ethic that would dampen the inflationary price expectations prevailing at the start of Phase II. [8] Establishing and maintaining such an ethic was made considerably more difficult for the commission by the failure of the Nixon Administration to provide the necessary moral support and leadership.

Although it did not begin its sharp on and off oscillations in controls policy until the end of Phase II, the Nixon Administration foreshadowed those swings and compromised the believability of controls

---

usually do so, however. For indirect admissions that cost-justification did not work as intended and that Phase II was unexpectedly bailed out by the profit-margin limitation, see U.S. Congress Joint Economic Committee, Hearings on Review of Phase II of the New Economic Program, April, 14, 18-21, 24, 1972, 92nd cong., 2nd sess. (Washington, D.C.: U.S. Government Printing Office, 1972), p. 24. For statements on Phase II as designed to deal with cost-push inflation and the need for a transition to Phase III to stop demand-pull inflation, see Economic Report of the President, 1973 (Washington, D.C.: U.S. Government Printing Office, 1973), pp. 69-70, 80; U.S. Congress Joint Economic Committee, Subcommittee on Consumer Economics, Hearings on the Cost of Living, March 21, April 4, May 8, 22, 23, 1973, 93rd cong., 1st sess. (Washington, D.C.: U.S. Government Printing Office, 1973), p. 6; U.S. Senate Committee on Banking, Housing and Urban Affairs, Hearings on Economic Stabilization Legislation–1973, January 29-31, February 1, 5-7, 1973, 93rd cong., 1st sess. (Washington, D.C.: U.S. Government Printing Office, 1974), p. 103.

throughout Phase II. Despite its lip service to the need for structural change in the economy, for instance, the Administration avoided such reforms as extended antitrust enforcement, reduced import restrictions, and improved farm policies, which would have been desirable in themselves and timely in fighting inflation. Similarly, it consummated a secret wheat sale to the Russians that even it subsequently admitted had negative implications for domestic price stability. [9] Although the Administration remained on the sidelines during Phase II in what it claimed was a stance of noninterference with the Price Commission, publicly confirmed by the commission chairman, the evidence shows that the Administration in fact thwarted a number of commission initiatives behind the scenes. While Council of Economic Advisors chairman Herbert Stein described the relationship between the Price Commission and the Cost of Living Council to Congress as "constructive," according to one of the Commissioners "there were several instances when Price Commission autonomy clashed with Cost of Living Council authority."[10] After interviewing a top-level Price Commission administrator following the transition to Phase III, one columnist reported "he maintains that everybody in the place who wanted to do a job was forced out or immobilized in the January switchover" when the White House "asked us to do things we didn't think were appropriate."[11]

EXPLAINING THE PRICE COMMISSION EXPERIENCE

Explaining why the Price Commission paid too little attention to economic analysis is not hard. First, the majority of the commissioners appointed by the president were not economists and did not always understand the economic nuances of the policies they promulgated or fully appreciated the need for technical economic analyses when choosing those policies. Second, the Price Commission chairman, not surprisingly, named mostly noneconomists with academic training and administrative experience similar to his own to the top positions on the commission staff. Third, these staffers in turn also hired mainly noneconomists, with the result that too few economists were hired in the face of resource constraints. Fourth, the commission experienced difficulties when it did seek to employ economists, since some who were sympathetic to the controls program were opposed to, and declined to work for, the Nixon Administration; others who supported the Administration either opposed controls, refused to be associated with them, or were unable to free themselves from other commitments and join the commission staff.

The possibility that the internal failings of the Price Commission were deliberate must be rejected. While hard data with which to document this conclusion are not available, my own involvement for most of

Phase II leaves me with no doubt that the Price Commission took its mission seriously and worked hard to slow inflation.* The striking majority of Price Commission staff members evidenced a high degree of job satisfaction and commitment. More than one rated his Price Commission job the best he had ever held in an informal discussion. Where dissatisfactions were expressed, special personal problems tended to be cited, and the Price Commission compared favorably to previous employment situations in most respects. A significant portion of commission employees were detailed there on temporary duty assignments by other federal government agencies, particularly in the initial stages of Phase II, when a staff had to be instantaneously assembled from scratch. Although other agencies had an incentive to deploy their least desirable personnel to the Price Commission, the levels of transferee effort and productivity seemed to exceed those typical of government employees. Most transferees remarked that they were more motivated and worked harder at the Price Commission than they had in their former positions and chose to remain at the commission when given the option upon expiration of their temporary duty assignments of returning to their old agencies.†

Explaining why the Nixon Administration failed to provide the Price Commission with adequate resources or support during Phase II is more difficult. At least three different theories with merit have been advanced. The Nixon Administration was ideologically opposed to controls; even after controls were adopted, internal disagreement about their proper

---

*I served full time as a consultant to the Price Commission on academic leave from January to September 1972.

†The Price Commission staff was not dedicated without reason. Two factors were especially important. First, the environment was exceptionally stimulating. The work in the first peacetime controls program ever, and the first controls program even in wartime for twenty years, afforded extensive interaction with many high-level corporate executives. It was new and involved a great deal of learning, and it required steering a highly visible course among many public interests. Second, the remunerative conditions were good, with uncommon opportunities for advancement and increased pay. The instantaneous creation of a bureaucracy from scratch, however temporary it was intended to be, required a large number of promotions purely for span of control and efficient management reasons. At the same time, civil service grade increases and salary boosts were needed to attract people to an organization that could offer relatively little job security. Many transferees were reluctant to go back to their old agencies because they would lose their higher civil service grades and associated prerequisites obtained at the Price Commission, even though their salaries could not be cut.

role persisted throughout the various freezes and phases. One possibility is that the lack of support provided to the Price Commission reflected nothing more than the fact that many within the Administration opposed controls and were reluctant to encourage the establishment of, or reliance on, a controls bureaucracy.

Controls were introduced by the Nixon Administration at the same time it suspended convertibility of the dollar and only a short time before it devalued the dollar. If controls were intended mainly as an external signal to foreign countries that the United States intended to do more about inflation than simply export it via exchange rate manipulations, then denying the Price Commission the resources and support needed to make Phase II effective internally would have made sense in light of the Administration's distaste for controls. Thus, a second possibility is that the 90-day freeze and Phase II represented a bid for foreign acceptance of nonconvertibility and devaluation never intended to have domestic significance.*

Critics of the Nixon Administration have offered still another, and less flattering, interpretation of Phase II as a political sham, which is that the controls were neither intended nor expected to slow inflation, but initiated solely to allow the Administration to pump up the economy temporarily prior to the 1972 elections without making inflation worse, creating the false impression among voters that everything possible was being done to stop inflation. If controls proved ineffective, as expected, the Democrats would be blamed for forcing them on the Administration; if controls somehow proved successful, the Administration would take credit for applying them. Although no solid evidence confirming this harsh assessment of Administration motives has been uncovered, such a view is not easily dismissed in light of the revelations of systematic corporate shakedowns and payoffs by the Committee to Reelect the President; the termination of the Price Commission and transition to Phase III just two months after the election; and the Watergate corruption. [12]

IMPLICATIONS FOR THE FUTURE

The Nixon Administration experimentation with wage and price controls did not provide a test of incomes policies in general, as some have suggested, but a test only of one specific series of actions. By

---

*Some members of the Nixon Administration have suggested off the record that controls were intended mainly for international show. See Arnold R. Weber, In Pursuit of Price Stability: The Wage-Price Freeze of 1971 (Washington, D.C.: The Brookings Institution, 1973), p. 7.

the time it finally gave up on controls in June 1974, the Nixon Administration had seriously eroded the credibility of mandatory incomes policies. Regardless of how Administration motives, objectives, and expectations for Phase II are diagnosed, two important lessons emerge from the history of the Price Commission. One concerns the need for technical analysis and expert judgment when setting policy involving complex issues. The other relates to the need for adequate resources and encouragement when starting new programs.

At the Price Commission, where economic analysis was often relegated to the background, the desire for administrative convenience led to the adoption of economically unsound policies such as the productivity, constant markup, and TLP policies discussed in the third section of this chapter, with inflationary results that negated the hard work of the commission staff. The commission might have adopted policies more effective in controlling inflation if it had recognized the need for expertise in economic analysis and hired additional economists. To be effective, future programs directed toward price control or similarly complex matters will have to integrate technical analysis into their decision structures and ensure the interaction of specialists with top administrators and policy makers to a greater extent than the Price Commission did.

To conclude that the Price Commission could have curbed inflation simply by adopting more suitable policies and regulations would be a mistake. Nixon Administration policies that worked at cross purposes to the controls program, and the failure of the Administration to provide the necessary resources or support, imposed serious external constraints on the Price Commission. Overcoming such burdens is difficult for any organization; for new and weak organizations lacking an established and firm base, they invariably take a heavy, if not fatal, toll in terms of programmatic success. To be effective, future controls efforts and other new governmental programs will require more nourishment in terms of resources and support than the Price Commission received from the Nixon Administration.

NOTES

1. For treatments of the European experience with incomes policies, see Allan Fels, The British Prices and Incomes Board, (London: Cambridge University Press, 1972); Organization for Economic Cooperation and Development, Inflation: The Present Problem (Paris: OECD, 1970); and Lloyd Ulman and Robert J. Flanagan, Wage Restraint: A Study of Incomes Policies in Western Europe (Berkeley: University of California Press, 1971).

2. Controls had been negatively evaluated by the Nixon Administration as early as 1970 in the annual report of the Council of Economic

Advisors and as recently as the end of July 1971 by the chairman of that
council in a letter to the Washington Post. See Economic Report of the
President, 1970 (Washington, D. C.: U. S. Government Printing Office,
1970), p. 23-24; Paul McCracken, "Galbraith and Price-Wage Controls,"
Washington Post (July 28, 1971), p. A-18.

3. Cost of Living Council, Executive Office of the President,
Economic Stabilization Program Quarterly Report: Covering the Period
August 15 through December 31, 1971 (Washington, D. C.: U. S. Govern-
ment Printing Office, 1972), pp. 115-18.

4. A. Bradley Askin and John Kraft, Econometric Wage and Price
Models: Assessing the Impact of the Economic Stabilization Program
(Lexington, Mass.: D. C. Heath, 1974), pp. 79-98; U. S. Senate
Committee on Commerce, Subcommittee for Consumers, Hearings on
Consumer Redress, August 16, 17, 20, and 21, 1973, 93rd cong.,
1st sess. (Washington, D. C.: U. S. Government Printing Office,
1973).

5. Mary T. Hamilton, "Price Controls in 1973: Strategies and
Problems," American Economic Review 64, no. 2 (May 1974): 100.

6. See Robert F. Lanzillotti and Blaine Roberts, "An Assessment
of the U. S. Experiment with an Incomes Policy," paper presented at the
Tulane Conference on Incomes Policies, New Orleans, April 1973;
Lanzillotti and Roberts, "The Legacy of Phase II Price Controls," American Economic Review 64, no. 2 (May 1974): 82-83.

7. For example, see Askin and Kraft, op. cit.; Robert J. Gordon,
"Wage-Price Controls and the Shifting Phillips Curves," Brookings
Papers on Economic Activity, no. 2 (1972), pp. 385-430.

8. The success of the Price Commission in creating such a
stabilization ethic is discussed in Lanzillotti and Roberts, "An Assessment of the U. S. Experiment with an Incomes Policy," op. cit., pp.
83-84; U. S. Senate Committee on Banking, Housing and Urban Affairs,
op cit., pp. 110-11.

9. "U. S. Admits Russia Got Best of Wheat Deal, Says Never
Again," Los Angeles Times (September 8, 1973), Part 1, p. 1.

10. See Lanzillotti and Roberts, "The Legacy of Phase II Price
Controls," op. cit., pp. 84-87; U. S. Congress Joint Economic Committee, Hearings on Review of Phase II of the New Economic Program,
op. cit., p. 12.

11. Nicholas Von Hoffman, "Two Anchovies in Every Pot," Washington Post (June 1, 1973), p. B-1.

12. For two very readable criticisms of the Nixon Administration
economic policies, see Roger Leroy Miller and Raburn M. Williams,
The New Economics of Richard Nixon: Freezes, Floats and Fiscal
Policy (San Francisco: Canfield Press, 1972); Leonard Silk, Nixonomics,
(2nd ed., New York: Praeger Publishers, 1973). Van Hoffman, op. cit.,
is also relevant.

CHAPTER

4

THE IMPACT AND ADMINISTRATION OF WAGE CONTROLS
Daniel J. B. Mitchell

THE RATIONALE FOR WAGE CONTROLS

Justification for direct controls in a market economy is always difficult in terms of conventional economic models. Monetary theory suggests a linkage between the nominal levels of wages and prices and the money supply, based on "real balances" or some other mechanism.[1] There is rather little theory available to define the tightness of that linkage or the speed with which it operates. If the linkage is believed to be "loose, " then the journalist's description of a "wage-price" spiral begins to make sense, and a possible justification for some instrument to intervene in the process develops. For the economist, however, there remains the problem of determining why the linkage might be loose, and for the policy maker there remains the need to uncover a "workable" instrument of intervention that produces more benefits than costs.

When economists, politicians, and policy makers speak of "incomes policy" or "wage-price controls, " union leaders often suspect that the concern is mainly "wages policy" and "wage controls, " and these suspicions are probably well grounded. An unspoken assumption often seems to be that if there is a loose linkage between traditional demand policy and the levels and movements of wages and prices, the looseness stems primarily from the labor market.

The labor market, particularly the collective bargaining sector, has always been something of a mystery to economists. There are references in the literature to a tendency of wages to be "sticky, " to a tendency of labor-management negotiations to come in "round, " and to the role of traditional ideas of "equity" and "coercive comparisons" in determining wages.[2] The inelegance of these notions evokes a

36

certain distaste among theoretical economists, but the notions are difficult for a pragmatist to ignore.

In the product market, by contrast, there is a well-developed economic theory of pricing. The standard textbook model assumes profit maximization as the goal of the firm and develops the cases of perfect competition and perfect monopoly, although, to be sure, the theory becomes rather vague when it enters the spectrum lying somewhere between these two extremes. Nevertheless, most economists believe that if demand and cost conditions remain pretty much the same, prices will remain reasonably stable. Prices may be kept relatively high in monopolistic situations, but once the target price is achieved stable demand and costs should lead to stable prices, even in the presence of monopoly. [3]

Of course, demand and cost conditions do not always remain the same. To the extent that an inflation stems primarily from improper demand (monetary and fiscal) policies, a correction in these policies is obviously warranted. However, if the problem stems from costs, demand policy may not produce the desired reaction. The key question is: Under what circumstances could an inflation stem from costs?

Most costs that face firms are simply prices charged by other firms. The major costly input that is not supplied by other firms is labor. For this reason, at an aggregate level, when the term "cost-push" inflation is used what is often meant is "wage-push." Furthermore, since a mechanism for "wage-push" is almost inconceivable in the nonunion sector, the main area of concern when "cost-push" inflation is discussed is collective bargaining settlements. In short, the lack of a theory of wage determination under collective bargaining leads to a suspicion that wage negotiations need not passively reflect demand conditions. All that can be said is that the process is "complex," that it depends on internal union political pressures, perceived equity in relative and absolute wages, and the willingness of employers to resist.

The will of employers to resist is of great importance. [4] But resistance depends heavily on expectations of future price behavior, that is, the future ability to recoup increased wage costs. Such expectations are unlikely to be determined in any simple way by current monetary and fiscal policy.

The wage emphasis was quite clear in the Economic Stabilization Program, which began in 1971. First-year wage rates in major construction-industry negotiations had risen 17.6 percent in 1970 in the face of rising unemployment rates in the industry. Even as the Administration continued to reject the general use of controls, direct regulation was imposed on wage settlements in unionized construction early in 1971. By August 1971 it had become apparent that the major nonconstruction union settlements were also not reacting to the slowing of the economy. First-year wage rate adjustments outside construction averaged 8.4

percent in 1969 and 10. 9 percent in 1970 and showed no signs of slowing down in 1971. Large settlements had already been reached in steel and telephones. For the first time in many years, a major longshore strike was underway on the West Coast; and the possibility of an East Coast dock strike was imminent. Congress was attempting to deal with a railroad bargaining impasse through emergency legislation, and the soft coal industry was nearing a negotiations deadlock. Labor-market jitters, in short, were a major factor behind the Administration's shift of ideological gears and imposition of controls.

Initially the new program froze most wages and prices. The goal was to break inflationary expectations, thereby stiffening employer resistance, and to provide a breathing space for planning the next phase. [5] The Phase II control system and the systems that followed showed a continuing wage emphasis. Price controls were based on markups and pass-throughs. If costs rose, prices could also rise; the major cost that was not a price was wages. Thus the success of the program hinged critically on its wage component.

THE IRONY OF WAGE CONTROLS

If wage jitters are often the primary motivation for interest in controls programs, why impose price controls? Why not have controls apply only to wages, as was initially done in 1971 in construction? The simple answer is that wage controls without price controls are unlikely to receive political support or union cooperation. Demands are quickly heard for controlling all forms of income, not just wages. Equal sacrifice becomes the slogan. George Meany, President of the AFL-CIO, stated in early 1972 that it had long been the official position of organized labor to cooperate with controls "providing . . . that the controls were fair and equitable, and that they were put on all segments of the economy that had any impact on the question of inflation."[6] In fact, of course, the objective of a controls program should be no sacrifices among large social groups. Income redistribution is not, or should not be, the objective. Distributional issues are better dealt with through taxes and transfer payments. The goal of controls is to make both wages and prices rise more slowly, and not to alter their relative rates of change.*

---

*In Europe controls are sometimes billed as a means of "planning" the income distribution; as a result, controls sometimes end up stimulating social tensions because of the politicization of incomes. For an example, see Daniel J. B. Mitchell, "Incomes Policy and the Labor Market in France," Industrial and Labor Relations Review 25 (April 1972),

The costs of controls are usually divided into administrative expenditures and economic distortions.* Administrative expenditures involve the payments to the bureaucrats who operate the program and for the materials, services, plant, and equipment they use. The costs borne by those who must comply with the regulations, involving the services of accountants, lawyers, and other professionals, also are part of the administrative costs. Economic distortions will vary in severity. † The most noticeable dislocations are product shortages, but less severe distortions can also occur. For example, sellers will seek ways of shifting costs to buyers, often in ways that may increase the total cost of the transaction. ‡

----

pp. 315-35. Even in Europe the emphasis is generally on the wage component of income; note the title of the recent book by Lloyd Ulman and Robert J. Flanagan on the subject: Wage Restraint: A Study of Incomes Policies in Western Europe (Berkeley: University of California Press, 1971).

*The Cost of Living Council provided Congress with a study of the administrative and distortionary costs of the Stabilization Program. Calculated at January 1974 salary rates, COLC estimated that the annual cost to the government of a Phase II effort would be $108 million, compared with $78 million for a Phase III effort and $100 million for a Phase IV effort. The annual cost to business of compliance was estimated at between $721 million and $2 billion. U.S. Senate Committee on Banking, Housing and Urban Affairs, Subcommittee on Production and Stabilization, "Statement of Dr. John T. Dunlop," 93rd cong., 2nd sess. February 6, 1974 (Washington, D.C.: Government Printing Office, 1974), p. 26 and Appendixes O and P.

†The National Association of Manufacturers published a study based on a poll of 2,300 member firms. A response rate of about 23 percent was obtained. The firms were asked whether controls had an adverse impact on various aspects of business practices. The results of the poll must be somewhat discounted because the NAM was engaged in a campaign to end controls at the time of the survey. It is not possible to quantify the results of the survey, but the NAM concluded that "controls have caused tremendous disruptions." Most of the disruptions cited involved the product market. Respondents claimed that employment had been adversely affected, but this appeared to be due to product shortages rather than wage controls. See National Association of Manufacturers, Industry Survey on Wage and Price Controls (Washington, D.C.: the Association, 1974).

‡My work with Professor Ross E. Azevedo indicates that inventories fell below the levels expected on the basis of business cycle factors during the Phase I-IV controls effort. Inventories can be viewed as a proxy for delivery reliability. The probably explanation is that firms cut costs by reducing the inventories of their own products, forcing their

It is possible for these distortions to appear in both the product
and labor markets. However, there appear to be differences in the
structural characteristics of the two markets that make product-market
distortions more likely. In the product market most buyers have little
incentive or ability to act as policemen, since their attachment to the
seller is often limited and tenuous.* Buyers generally cannot be certain
about the legality of a price, since only detailed accounting data can
determine whether the price is in compliance with the rules. In the labor
market, however, buyers and sellers are more firmly attached. The
buyer has every incentive—as well as the information necessary—to act
as policeman. Only if wage controls are so restrictive that labor shortages occur will both buyer and seller have a mutual interest in cheating.
Such a development is unlikely, since controls on wages are generally
aimed mainly at the union sector, where wages are above "market"
levels. Thus moderate wage restraint is unlikely to produce a shortage.

Viewed in this context, the distribution of the costs of controls is
rather ironic. A major motivation behind controls is concern with the
behavior of the labor market, and price controls are established along
with wage controls mainly in order to gain support for the wage program;
yet the burden of costs falls mainly on the product market, not on the
labor market.

TYPES OF WAGE CONTROLS

Wage controls can be administered on a comprehensive basis with
broad coverage and widespread mandatory compliance, or they can be
tailored to deal with the problems of a few special situations. The
controls that began in 1971 had both elements. Selective programs
were established to deal with wages in construction and later in food
and health. Because controls of the selective type deal with a relatively small universe, they can be tailored to meet specific sectoral
needs. If labor-market problems are felt to cover a broad range of
industries, the micro-level approach could become very expensive.
Comprehensive controls of the Phase II type are forced to rely on general guidelines that can readily be applied across the board.

---

customers to either maintain inventories or put up with increased
waiting time for new orders.

*Rents are an exception to this, since buyers and sellers are
more tightly linked in the housing market than elsewhere. The Internal
Revenue Service received 65,826 rent complaints during Phase II.
(Data supplied to the author by the IRS.)

Apart from food, health, and construction, the wage controls that operated during Phases III and IV fall somewhere between the comprehensive and selective models. In general the broad Phase II guidelines were de-emphasized, and special attention was paid to pattern-setting settlements in whatever industries happened to be negotiating. Outside the sectors designated for selective controls, and the key settlements, the labor market was left to "self-administer."

Each model of wage controls has its drawbacks. A comprehensive program is forced to issue some sort of wage standard, such as the Pay Board's 5.5 percent guideline. As critics have pointed out, such guidelines are inevitably somewhat arbitrary and may be inappropriate in some circumstances.* To handle the more apparent inequities, general exceptions can be formulated. Examples can be found in the Pay Board's rules for "catch up," tandem relationships, and labor shortages. Even with exceptions, however, guidelines cannot fit every situation. As a result, some procedure to review individual cases must be provided.

Selective controls require a great deal of cooperation from both sides of the bargaining table if they are to succeed. The case-by-case reviews that such controls entail imply a relatively high administrative cost per case. In addition, like other regulatory agencies that are concerned with a specific industry, there is always a danger that an industry wage board may become the captive of those it was designed to regulate.†

Finally, the intermediate model of Phases III and IV, which concentrated on the "key" settlements, poses two major issues. First, the behind-the-scenes dealing that such an approach involves raises some fundamental questions about the proper role of government regulation.

---

*A critique of the numerical guidelines approach can be found in D. Quinn Mills, "Problems in Formulating a General Pay Standard," Monthly Labor Review 97 (March 1974), pp. 31-34. Mills's criticism carries forth one of the elements in the controversy between the Pay Board and the Construction Industry Stabilization Committee. He argues that a general guideline cannot take account of wage structure. As a result, distortions of wage differentials may not be corrected and inflationary pressures will continue. The Pay Board accepted CISC's wage structure approach for construction, but did not think it feasible in an economywide program with widespread mandatory reporting.

†Apart from the policy issue noted in the previous footnote, part of the Pay Board versus CISC controversy stemmed from fears of members of the board that CISC would begin to "drift" from its objectives. It was feared that the balancing needed to maintain tripartitism at CISC might lead to insufficient wage restraint in construction unless there were outside, that is, Pay Board, monitoring and pressure.

Deals that are made outside the public view are not available for public
scrutiny. The danger of abuse of both due process and the public interest
cannot be ignored. Second, if controls are centered on settlements that
are believed to be pattern setters, it is unknown how long such settlements will continue to be viewed as leaders. If only the leaders are
subject to official scrutiny, might not the followers begin to look elsewhere for leadership? In short, wage controls based only on key settlements could begin to erode.

ADMINISTRATIVE ASPECTS OF WAGE CONTROLS

Comprehensive Wage Controls: The Phase II Experience

Administration

The Phase II Pay Board provides a unique look at the problems of
administering direct wage controls on a comprehensive basis. At the
end of Phase II the board had a staff of about 240 full- and part-time
employees. This staff was required to deal with the caseload generated
by Category I and II employee units, those units with 1,000 or more
workers, which had to report all adjustments to the Pay Board directly.*
The staff also had to handle appeals from the smaller Category III units,
after these cases were initially processed by the Internal Revenue Service. In addition, nonunion construction and executive compensation
cases were also the responsibility of the Pay Board. Also, of course,
aside from casework, the staff prepared policy papers; followed general
economic trends; and dealt with the press, Congress, and the public.

"Start up" costs in administering the Pay Board's comprehensive
wage control system were high. The board itself, because of its tripartite composition, had to pass through a very painful policy-making
stage during the early months of its program. What staff there was had
to walk a delicate line to avoid offending any of the three blocs on the
board. Initially, however, the main problem was the absence of a permanent staff for the first six weeks or so after Phase II began. Instead,

---

*The Bureau of Labor Statistics estimated that about 19 million
workers were in Category I and II units. However, some of these were
state and local employees, who did not have to report unless exceptions
were requested. Thus about 15 to 16 million workers in Categories I
and II regularly reported to the Pay Board. See Victor J. Sheifer,
"Reconciling Labor Department and Stabilization Agency Wage Data,"
Monthly Labor Review 96 (April 1973), pp. 24-30.

a revolving group of "detailees" from other government agencies attempted to service the board. The tripartite Pay Board was in no condition to worry about the situation.

The permanent staff began to form early in 1972 after the appointment of an executive director. These new appointees tended to be relatively young and inexperienced, the very type of people who are willing to work long hours in a crisis atmosphere at an agency with an uncertain life expectancy. Surprisingly, the level of competence of the professional staff was quite high. The weakest areas at the beginning were in what should have been routine functions: mail was not delivered properly, resulting in case-processing delays; personnel records were lost, delaying new hirings. The Pay Board was nearly eight months old before its computer could provide useful management and economic data. Eventually, all of these problems had to be dealt with by internal management reshuffles. Naturally, the service that could be provided to applicants and the public was limited until they were resolved.

An understanding of these "start up" costs is critical to an evaluation of the administrative performance of the Pay Board. First, the Board's difficulties underscore the problems that inevitably result if a comprehensive wage control system is started from scratch on short notice. Second, in analyzing the data for Phase II case processing, it is important to keep in mind that the board was not in a "steady state" for many months after it was created.

As has already been noted, a comprehensive program of the Phase II type had to rely on general rules that did not require case-by-case approvals. A guideline of 5.5 percent for wages was established for "new" situations, those negotiated or determined during Phase II. A 7 percent standard was applied in "old" situations, those that were set forth in contracts written prior to Phase II but scheduled to occur during it. Additional amounts above the standards were allowed for "qualified" fringe benefits. Exceptions allowing adjustments up to 7 percent in new cases were permitted on the basis of criteria spelled out in the regulations. Units seeking more than allowed by the standards and exceptions had to request special approval.

Category I and II units reported directly to the board even if they made wage adjustments that were clearly within the standards. Cases in Categories I and II could be divided into three classifications. First, cases that were within the standards could be "turned around" quickly, after only an arithmetic check. Second, there were exception requests which the staff had authority to adjudicate; these were primarily cases that met the board's formula exceptions or were tandem to previous board decisions. Third, there were requests that the staff had no authority to grant. These would be sent to a subtribunal of the board, the Cases and Appeals Panel. Within this class were the "big" cases, such as longshoring and railroads. Such specially important cases received elaborate staff preparation (once a staff was available) and often involved public hearings by the full Pay Board.

Category III units were not required to report adjustments to the board unless an exception request was sought. If reports for all adjustments had been required, the wage program would have simply been buried in an avalanche of cases, even after the small-employer exemption was implemented. The rule that only exception requests had to be filed, substantially limited the case volume. Roughly three-fourths of the private labor force was in Category III initially, but not more than 2 million Category III workers ever came into direct contact with the stabilization program. Category III cases generally were sent by the parties to the Internal Revenue Service for processing and reached the Pay Board mainly through appeals.

The Pay Board closed about 13,800 case submissions in its processing system during its existence.* About 10 percent of these were nonunion construction cases; about 17 percent were executive compensation cases; 34 percent were Category I and II submissions; and the remaining 39 percent were Category III. However, for reasons described below, the Category III record does not represent the full amount of Category III work completed at the board level.

Category I and II cases involved the bulk of the workers coming in contact with the Stabilization Program. About 15 to 16 million workers had to report regularly to the Pay Board in these categories. (See the footnote at the beginning of this section.) Table 4.1 provides sample summary data on processing time for those cases, based on computer records maintained by the Pay Board. Mean processing time from arrival at the board to "closing" was 43 days for "new" cases, those involving adjustments determined or negotiated during Phase II, and 63 days for "old" cases.† It should be noted that a delay in reviewing an "old" case did not necessarily mean that the workers affected received delayed payments. If the board did not meet its own specified processing deadline, payments could begin on schedule. A delayed

---

*These figures were drawn from Pay Board/Cost of Living Council computer records as of March 12, 1973, for Phase II cases. Each submission is counted as a "case" even if the request was withdrawn prior to decision.

†These figures cover all cases closed through January 12, 1973, that had complete data on date of receipt and date of closing. "Closing" a case usually occurred a day or two after the decision was mailed to the applicant; hence the processing time is slightly exaggerated by the use of the closing date. The Pay Board continued to close Phase II cases after Phase III began, but the processing time had been reduced through various short cuts in order to bring down the backlog prior to the board's termination date (February 28, 1973). Thus, Phase II cases closed during Phase III have been excluded because the processing time did not represent normal procedures.

TABLE 4.1

Sample of Pay Board Cases for which
Duration Data are Available, Categories I and II

| | Percent of Cases by Duration | |
	Old Cases	New Cases
Duration (in days)		
10 or less	6.5	6.5
11-20	12.8	21.4
21-30	15.2	25.0
31-40	11.4	12.3
41-50	10.1	10.0
51-100	25.8	14.8
More than 100	18.1	10.0
Total	100.0	100.0
Number of cases in sample	1,118	2,341
Mean duration	63 days	43 days

Note: Includes cases closed through January 12, 1973, for which
data on arrival date and closing date were available.
Source: Pay Board computer records.

rollback decision simply meant that a downward adjustment in the wage
to the approved level had to be made after the decision. Refunds of
previous excess payments were not required.

Table 4.2 provides duration data by selected closing dates.
(Closing of cases occurred on Fridays, for all cases that had a decision
mailed out during the week.) The record indicates some progress toward
reducing the processing time of Category I and II "new" cases. This
progress was probably the result of the computerized costing system
introduced towards the end of Phase II. The system allowed an auto-
mated turnaround of cases that fell within the basic standards, sometimes in a single day.* "Old" cases had a lower susceptibility toward

---

*The computer was programmed to kick out cases that had peculiar
characteristics for a human check. In general, however, the figures
provided by applicants were taken at face value. Major cases such
as the longshore cases were given closer scrutiny, and IRS audits were
requested in a few instances.

TABLE 4. 2

Duration of Cases by Selected Closing Date,
Categories I and II

Closing Date	Mean Duration (in days)	
	New Cases	Old Cases
August 25, 1972	39	63
September 29, 1972	37	73
October 27, 1972	55	67
November 24, 1972	38	75
December 29, 1972	29	76
January 12, 1973	31	52
Total*	43	63

*Includes cases closed through January 12, 1973 for which data on arrival date and closing date were available.

Source: Pay Board computer records.

quick decision and automation. The Pay Board regarded such cases as highly sensitive and was reluctant to provide the staff with a strong delegation of authority to deal with them.

Apart from the computer system, attempts were made to speed up case processing by improving the management of the procedure. Cases that required "adjudication," that is, that required exceptions to the standards, were handled in the Case Management and Analysis office. At first cases were passed from adjudicator to adjudicator within that office as various aspects of the submission were considered, but this assembly-line method tended to dilute the responsibility of any one adjudicator for the development of a case. It was decided, therefore, to switch to a team approach, in which a group of adjudicators headed by a team leader had responsibility for a case during much of its processing life. The experiment was reminiscent of those industrial job enlargement techniques in which a team is made responsible for the entire construction of an automobile or other product.

Internal worksheets were maintained by the Pay Board staff concerning the backlog of cases. The last surviving sheet was dated December 14, 1972 (one month before the end of Phase II), and indicates a total backlog of 1, 336 cases.* Of these, 352 were Category I and II

*During much of Phase II, the Pay Board issued a weekly press release giving data on the weighted average approval in Categories I

submissions; 501 were Category III cases that had gotten beyond the Category III Panel; 45 were nonunion construction; and 438 were executive compensation. The overall backlog figure had been moving down up until that date, although much of the progress simply reflected a shifting of Category III cases from the regular case-processing system to the Category III Panel.

In the early days of Phase II the IRS had no authority concerning Category III cases, other than to receive them. In effect IRS simply operated as a mail drop for the board until it was delegated limited authority to approve the formula exceptions; once this authority was granted, the pendulum swung in the other direction. The system required that even cases in which the IRS had no authority to grant exceptions had to move through the IRS procedures in order to receive the inevitable denial. They were then eligible for an appeal to the Pay Board. Eventually the board acted to provide for direct shunting of such cases into its own case mechanism.

Because of the substantial volume of Category III appeals from the IRS, the board was forced to establish a staff-operated Category III Panel. This panel issued advisory opinions to the chairman of the Pay Board. The Category III Panel heard only cases for which Pay Board precedents were available. Others were referred to the Pay Board and its subtribunal. Under an informal arrangement, the Teamsters alternate screened all panel decisions and could certify cases about which he disagreed with the decisions of the Pay Board for review. By the end of Phase II the panel had heard 1,812 exception requests and 185 appeals from its own decisions.* The panel existed for 25 weeks during Phase II and probably met about twice a week. Since this works out to about 40 cases per day, it is evident that substantial time could not be devoted to each case. In general, IRS personnel prepared the summary

---

and II. Included was an estimate of the backlog calculated by subtracting decisions issued from cases received. Unfortunately there were channels by which cases could enter the board without being recorded through normal procedures, so the inflow-outflow estimate was highly unreliable. For internal management, an actual count of cases was initiated. Some cases were missed even by this procedure, since case adjudicators were under great pressure to keep their personal backlogs down and some tended to "hide" cases as a result. In addition there was a certain amount of negotiation between the Executive Director and the Case Management and Analysis Office over exactly what was considered to be in the backlog. These problems in obtaining reliable managerial data were symptomatic of the general lack of resources for handling case processing.

*Including the period after the end of Phase II, the Category III panel processed 3,331 cases.

reports given to the panel concerning each case. These summaries were
not prepared with the same care that went into summaries accompanying
Category I and II cases. The relative limitation of information provided
to the Category III Panel was aggravated by the fact that incomplete
data often arrived with Category III cases, partly because the small
units involved were inexperienced in dealing with federal programs.

The Phase II mechanisms for processing Category III were in danger
of being swamped by the volume. In an instinctive protective reaction
the handling of Category III was separated from the regular case mechanism at the Pay Board level. Cases awaiting the Category III Panel were
not counted as part of the board's backlog, although the number of
pending cases must have been substantial. Of the some 15,683 cases
received by IRS during Phase II, almost one-third (5,021) were withdrawn, mainly because it turned out that no exception was required. [7]
But the limited authority of the IRS to approve exceptions ensured that
many of the remaining cases eventually wound up at the board. The
IRS sent 2,096 cases to the board directly and another 1,296 after an
initial denial; IRS records indicate that 2,293 other cases were denied
on final appeal within the IRS and that many of these were probably then
submitted to the board by the applicants. There was every incentive
for applicants to file appeals: once a case had been prepared, the
marginal cost of appealing was the price of a first-class letter.

Some estimate of the magnitude of the Category III problem can be
seen on Table 4.3, which shows the results of a random sample of 101
cases decided by the Category III Panel during Phase II. * It indicates
that the mean time elapsed from initial filing with the IRS to appeal to
the Pay Board was 90 days; another 114 days elapsed on average from
the filing of the appeal to the board to the mailing of the board's decision; thus it took an average of 204 days to process a case in the sample
through an initial decision of the Category III Panel. Appeals that were
certified from the panel to the board could take even longer. Delays of
such lengths in Category III cases were obviously not consistent with
the Pay Board's own goal of due process. †

---

*Computer records were not kept on Category III Panel cases. As
a result, a random sample had to be drawn from the boxes in which the
cases were later stored. The sample represents 5.6 percent of the
universe of cases processed by the panel during Phase II.

†Of course, some lawyers might find such delays short when
compared with the current waiting times in some courts. However, in
the context of collective bargaining the delay would create a considerable inconvenience. Parties would find themselves negotiating second
control-year contracts while still awaiting a decision concerning what
the base wage could be for the first year.

TABLE 4. 3

Category III Processing Time during Phase II

Duration (in days)	From Application to IRS to Appeal to Pay Board (in percent)	From Appeal to Pay Board to Mailing of Decision (in percent)	Duration (in days)	From Application to IRS to Mailing of Decision (in percent)
1-30	8	1	1-60	0
31-60	19	8	61-120	5
61-90	28	29	121-180	41
91-120	24	23	181-240	26
121-150	12	18	241-300	18
151-180	3	14	301-360	11
Over 180	7	8	Over 361	0
Total	100	100	Total	100
Mean duration	90 days	114 days	Mean duration	204 days

Source: Sample of 101 Category III cases closed during Phase II.

Dealing with the caseload problem would have required either a less comprehensive program, as Phase III turned out to be, or a larger staff. At the Pay Board level it is unlikely that further innovations could have increased productivity. The computer system and the team system were in place. The members of the Pay Board were not full-time officials, and it is doubtful that much could have been done to increase their availability for hearing cases. Possibly something could have been done to improve efficiency at the IRS level. Since stabilization was not part of the normal career pattern for IRS employees, the incentives provided IRS personnel to work in the stabilization program were weak. On the other hand, the IRS did have local offices available for stabilization when the Pay Board was created. The alternative of requiring the board to establish and maintain its own local offices would have imposed such a tremendous burden that it could not have been justified for a short-run effort. *

---

*As might be expected, frictions sometimes arose between the IRS and the Pay Board. The board's staff complained about the rapid turnover of IRS case processors, which made continual training programs necessary. On the other side, IRS staff were demoralized by the exceptions granted by the board in the early major cases and by the slowness that characterized the board's establishment of policy decisions.

Policing

Any comprehensive wage control effort that imposes rules and reporting requirements on large numbers of units needs some method of promoting compliance. In some instances "moral suasion" and public pressure may be sufficient to induce "voluntary" cooperation; but generally, more direct policing is needed if the program is to have credibility.

Legal enforcement of wage controls raises a touchy public relations issue. Agencies that force rollbacks on "price gougers" are bound to receive favorable publicity. Hauling employers into court for paying too-high wages, however, is unlikely to bring public accolades. Indeed, public cooperation in reporting wage violations is likely to be limited. The Phase II record indicates that the IRS received almost 156,000 complaints, but only about 4,000 of these concerned wages. The others involved prices and rents. [8] When wage complaints were received from the public, they were often in connection with pay increases of public officials that had been reported in the press. Aside from this special category of complaints, it is evident that a compliance-enforcement program for comprehensive wage controls involves the seeking out of violators.

About one-fourth of the wage investigations, pending or closed, of the IRS as of September 13, 1972, were the result of outside complaints. The others developed as the result of IRS audits (often originally intended to pick up price violations) or through other channels.* Some selective spot-checking was done on the wage side by IRS, mostly in connection with the executive-compensation rules. Management-consulting firms and financial institutions were subject to especially intensive sweeps, because such firms have many contacts in the business world; it was thought that through these contacts they would spread the word about the "toughness" of the compliance effort. A program was established whereby the parties to expiring collective bargaining contracts were telephoned and asked if they had submitted the required reports. Neither of these efforts uncovered many violations, but the intent was to create the impression that someone was watching, not to lock up "wage gougers."

Actual courtroom litigation under the Phase II wage compliance program was quite limited. In one case an injunction was obtained forbidding a strike of a handful of warehouse employees against the wage

---

*Reports on compliance investigations were generally confidential. The September 13, 1972, report, however, survived in the Pay Board's files. This unpublished report was produced by the Cost of Living Council and was entitled Compliance Investigation Status Report and Watch List.

program. * This case was unique bacause of the almost complete absence
of strikes against controls. In another court action, the principle of
not permitting disallowed wage increases to be paid into escrow for
disbursement when the program ended was upheld.† A number of other
court cases simply dissipated and were dropped before final action was
taken.

Although IRS field agents seemed anxious to pursue technical violations, the Pay Board and the Cost of Living Council were not enthusi-
astic about conducting legal battles with small employers, who often
ran afoul of the rules inadvertently. The Justice Department, which
handled the government's side, was even more reluctant to take on any
cases that did not have a very high probability of being won. IRS field
agents were reportedly demoralized by the lack of enforcement litigation,
but the alternative would have been a substantial shift of resources to
legal battles with little payoff.

Less Comprehensive Programs
and the Phase III and Phase IV Experience

In terms of resource commitment it is difficult to develop comparisons between Phase II procedures and less comprehensive efforts at
controls, since "less comprehensive" covers a broad range of options.
However, some comparisons can be made with the Phase III and IV effort.
Even on that basis, the fact that the wage and price functions were
merged after Phase II makes separation of the two types of controls
impossible. Moreover, considerable effort was spent after Phase II in
clearing up the backlog of Phase II business. Therefore, some post-
Phase II resources should really be charged to Phase II.

According to the Cost of Living Council, 4, 039 employees were
required to man the entire Phase II apparatus. This dropped to 2, 800
in Phase III and 3, 700 in Phase IV. [9] The main difference between
Phases II and IV was on the wage side, so that the move toward selective controls plus the key settlements appears to have dropped the
overall requirements of the program by something over 300 employees.
This method of estimation seems reasonable, since the drop in employ-

---

*The strike at the Crescent Warehouse Company of Los Angeles
was called over the employer's insistence on a clause in the contract
providing that he was not obligated to exceed the increment allowable
under Pay Board rules. Eighteen employees were involved.

†The case involved an attempt by Los Angeles electricians to have
a disallowed deferred adjustment paid into an escrow account. A decision by federal district court supporting the government's position was
later upheld by the Temporary Emergency Court of Appeals.

ment was essentially at the IRS, which had had to process Category III wage cases in Phase II. Category III was essentially removed from the program in the self-administered sectors after Phase II.

The Cost of Living Council reports having received 11, 219 wage cases through January 24, 1974, that related to Phase III and IV adjustments. Only about one-fifth of these cases involved the self-administered sector and executive compensation. The rest came from food, health, and nonunion construction, the selective control areas. [10] These figures simply reinforce the saving in administrative resources that can be achieved by using less comprehensive wage controls. The Pay Board and IRS received a substantially higher case inflow in Phase II, even when adjusted for the relative durations of the phases. *

As noted earlier, the key problem for a wage control effort is to determine the appropriate balance between a totally comprehensive program and a limited program. There are also issues regarding the appropriate degree of comprehensiveness at various stages of the program. Should wage controls begin at a highly comprehensive level and then be narrowed on an iterative basis to problem areas and key settlements, or can the program operate selectively from the beginning? The advantage of the former option is that it helps pinpoint the areas in which problems seem to be centered. Its disadvantage is the large amount of redundant administrative work created.

MEASURING THE IMPACT OF WAGE CONTROLS

A standard approach in evaluating programs of direct controls has been to estimate some sort of wage equation using the precontrol period as the period of observation. The equation is then used to predict the rate of wage change during the controls period. An overprediction (actual wage increase below predicted increase) is deemed a "success" of the program, or at least a sign that the program had an impact. This technique was popularized by George Perry's well-known study of the Kennedy-Johnson guideposts and has been used with variations since that time to evaluate U. S. and foreign experiments with controls. [11]

Although there are flaws in the practical application of Perry's residual methodology, it appears to ask the right question: How does the world with controls compare with the world as it would have been without controls? The technique appears to be sophisticated because

---

*During the 14 months of Phase II the IRS received 15, 683 cases, while the Pay Board closed 8, 410 cases other than Category III. Thus, about 24, 000 cases were received by the wage program as a whole, and the annual rate of case intake during Phase II was roughly double the Phase III-IV annual rate. (These figures exclude the Construction Industry Stabilization Committee.)

it avoids the pitfall of simple before-and-after comparisons; that is, the existence of forces besides controls that influence wage determination is recognized. Unfortunately, the residual technique is inappropriate for the controls program that began in 1971.

The best way to examine the methodological issue is to consider the difference between the Kennedy-Johnson guideposts, to which the original Perry study applied, and the Economic Stabilization Program. The guideposts were designed to keep inflation "below normal" so that the economy could be further stimulated through monetary and fiscal policy. As Sheahan describes the atmosphere when the Kennedy administration took over, "On all the available evidence, a greater rate of economic expansion could be expected to stimulate wage claims and to reduce the restraint on price increases. . . . The answer attempted . . . was the system of wage-price guideposts."[12] In other words, the probable result of expansion would be inflationary, and the administration was seeking to find some instrument to cope with this anticipated relationship.

In contrast to the Sheahan description concerning the formulation of the guideposts, consider the description of the period prior to the 1971 controls, as it appeared in the 1973 Economic Report of the President:

> There were several reasons why the rate of inflation might continue to decline (without controls). First, prices and wages would be responding, with a lag, to the slowdown in the economy that had occurred earlier. Second, the prospective recovery of the economy . . . would still leave the economy in a situation of excess demand . . . throughout 1972. Third, more rapid recovery would accelerate the rise of productivity . . . .
>
> On the other hand, there were reasons why the inflation rate which had been declining since 1969 . . . might accelerate. . . . Even if the more pessimistic outcome was actually unlikely, there was widespread fear of it, and this fact was itself important . . . .
>
> The controls were intended to deal with the risk that inflation would again accelerate. To reduce that risk . . . was a very significant contribution, but one that would not necessarily show up in a reduction of the inflation rate below what would most probably have occurred without the controls.[13]

The Economic Stabilization Program, in short, was not intended to alter the essential structure of wage and price determination at the economy-wide level. Although certain elements of the wage program, the selective control areas such as construction, were designed to change "normality," most of the program was an insurance policy against a deviation from normality. For economists attempting to determine the effectiveness of controls, this feature of the program is most unsettling. It is impossible to tell whether the program was a success or a failure simply by noting whether precontrol models predict or overpredict wage developments during controls.

A second problem in using aggregate models to evaluate controls on the wage side follows from the fact that wage controls were really aimed at a narrow group, those units in the collective bargaining sector that were negotiating new contracts. Table 4.4 provides summary data on Pay Board average requests and approvals in Category I and II wage cases.[14] The only area where cutbacks were appreciable on an aggregate basis was that of new union contracts.* Nonunion units and units with deferred adjustments established prior to controls were virtually unaffected by rollbacks, although of course there were some cutbacks in all sectors. Workers under expiring contracts accounted for roughly one-fourth of the major union labor force during 1972 and about 45 percent in 1973. As a whole, less than 30 percent of nonfarm employment is unionized. The hope was that by bringing new union settlements

TABLE 4.4

Pay Board Weighted Average Requests and Grants,
Categories I and II, Phase II Cases

Type of Case	Average Request	Average Grant
All cases	5.6	5.4
Union cases	6.2	5.9
New union cases	7.6	6.9
Nonunion cases	5.0	4.9
Cases cut back*	10.3	7.6

*Cases in which the recorded requests exceeds the grant.
Source: Pay Board computer records as of March 2, 1973.

---

*The average approval by the Construction Industry Stabilization Committee during Phase II was about 5.7 percent, but no data are available on the average request coming to CISC or the craft boards that initially screened CISC cases. The Cost of Living Council did not issue comparable data on wage adjustments reported and approved during Phases III and IV.

down to a level in keeping with general economic forces and noninfla-
tionary expectations, the possibility of staying within the normal range
of price determination would be enhanced. However, the short-run
effects of influencing a portion of a minority of the labor force is likely
to be lost in the general noise of aggregate economic data series and
may be undetectable by econometric wage equations.

Measurement problems are encountered even when what is sought
is the simple answer to what actually happened, rather than what would
have been. The appendix to this chapter reviews some of these data
problems and notes the particular measurement problem posed by Social
Security payroll tax changes that occurred during controls. While it
would be better to be more precise, it appears difficult to say more
than that the underlying rates of wage and fringe change during 1972
and 1973 were in the lower 6 percent and lower 7 percent ranges, respectively. Attempts to look at periods of less than one year are not very
informative, since the program imposed new timing (seasonal) patterns.

Table 4.5 indicates that first-year wage adjustments under major
union settlements were running in the 11 to 12 percent range during the
precontrol period, essentially the years ending with 1971. During 1972
(Phase II) a marked drop occurred in the major settlements. The downward trend continued into Phases III and IV (1973), although creative
use of escalators and fringes tends to understate the more recent figures.
An interesting question is why the settlements were so high during the
precontrol period. Was something occurring that would have justified
the fears of a deviation from normality in the union sector?

Wage equations can be used to examine the immediate precontrol
period to see if wage changes appeared to be running at an above-normal
rate. Previous research in this area does not provide unambiguous evidence at an aggregate level.[15] Residuals from some wage equations
tend to be positive (actual minus predicted), while in others no substantial deviations occur. If the analysis is confined to the union
sector, there is some evidence of positive residuals, followed by a
return to normal during Phase II. However, wage data for the union
sector are extremely crude when series that are available for a long
period of time are used.[16]

There is some evidence that part of the explanation for the rapid
wage increases that were negotiated prior to controls was that they
were the result of a catching-up process. Table 4.6 presents a sectoral analysis of wage changes over the period 1965-73. Sector A
consists of those industries that received less than the median increase
in average hourly earnings during 1972; Sector B consists of those
industries that received more.* The table indicates that Sector B tended

---

*Sector A industries are ordnance; food; tobacco; apparel; lumber;
furniture; printing and publishing; rubber; leather; electrical equipment;

TABLE 4. 5

Percent of Change in Wage Rates
in Major Union Settlements, 1970-72

	1970	1971	1972	(preliminary) 1973
Wage rates alone (1, 000 or more workers)				
First-year change				
All industries	11.9	11.6	7.3	5.8
Construction	17.6	12.6	6.9	5.2
Nonconstruction	10.9	11.6	7.4	5.9
Life-of-contract*				
Construction	14.9	10.8	6.0	5.2
Nonconstruction	7.9	7.9	6.5	5.2
All industries	8.9	8.1	6.4	5.2
Contracts with escalators	7.3	7.1	5.7	4.9
Contracts without escalators	10.1	9.2	6.5	5.4
Wages and benefits (5, 000 or more workers)				
First-year change in all industries	13.1	13.1	8.5	7.1
Life-of-contract* in all industries	9.1	8.8	7.4	6.1

*Excludes cost-of-living escalator adjustments.
Source: Bureau of Labor Statistics, Current Wage Developments,
various issues.

to include the higher-paying, heavily unionized industries. It appears
from Table 4. 6 that the industries that tended to receive "more" during
Phase II had also tended to receive "less" in the late 1960s.

---

miscellaneous manufactures; wholesale and retail trade; finance, insurance, and real estate; and services. Sector B consists of textiles;
paper; chemicals; petroleum; stone, clay, and glass; fabricated metals;
primary metals; machinery; transportation equipment; professional instruments; mining and quarrying; construction; transportation; telephone and
telegraph; utilities.

TABLE 4.6

Sectoral Developments

| | | Sector B[b] | | |
	Sector A[a]	Including Construction	Excluding Construction	All Industries
Annual rate of change in average hourly earnings (in percent)				
1965-70	5.8	5.4	5.0	5.7
1971	6.0	8.4	8.5	6.7
1972	5.6	8.2	8.5	6.4
1973	6.4	6.8	7.0	6.5
Annual employment growth (in percent)				
1972	3.9	3.8	4.9	3.9
1973	3.3	4.7	4.0	3.7
Unionization rate, 1970 (in percent)	18.6	58.5	54.5	31.6
Average hourly earnings, December 1971 (in dollars)	3.11	4.46	4.11	3.51
Increase in after-tax profits[c] (in percent)				
1971-72	15.7	16.8	16.7	16.4
1972-73	12.3	28.9	28.9	23.1

[a]Industries that received less than the median increase in average hourly earnings during 1972.

[b]Industries that received more than the median increase in average hourly earnings during 1972.

[c]Profit data exclude ordnance.

Source: Earnings and employment growth calculated on a December-to-December basis, using industry data; the percent of change in earnings was weighted by December 1971 employment levels; earnings and employment data are from Employment and Earnings; the unionization rate is the number of union and employee association members in 1970 from Directory of National Unions and Employee Associations 1971, divided by 1970 payroll employment; profit figures are calculated from First National City Bank Newsletter, April 1973 and April 1974.

TABLE 4.7

Mean Annual Rate of Wage Increase Experienced
under Major Contracts Expiring in 1973
(in percent)

	All Durations[a]	One-Year Contracts[b]	Two-Year Contracts[c]	Three-Year Contracts[d]
Nonconstruction	8.9	7.0	9.1	9.0
Manufacturing	7.4	6.3	8.1	6.8
Nonmanufacturing, excluding construction	10.7	7.3	10.5	11.5
Construction	11.0	7.3	11.3	11.9
All Contracts	9.1	7.1	9.3	9.3

[a]Less than 48 months or more than 12 months, not shown separately.
[b]Less than 24 months but more than 12 months.
[c]Less than 36 months but more than 24 months.
[d]Less than 48 months but more than 36 months.
Source: Based on special tabulations provided to the Pay Board by the Bureau of Labor Statistics, appearing in Pay Board Staff Paper OCE-99, November 22, 1972. Estimates include cost-of-living escalator adjustments.

Various factors might be cited to explain the tendency for the union sector to have lagged behind in the late 1960s. Unanticipated inflation combined with long-term contracts would tend to produce a wage lag. There may even have been some residual effect of the old Kennedy-Johnson guideposts involved. Phase II had certain elements that were conducive to catching up, or even overshooting. Employment growth was more rapid in Sector B, outside construction, than in Sector A, and the Sector B profit picture was relatively brighter.

By 1973 the gap between the rates of increase in earnings of the two sectors was narrowing. This narrowing might also be explained in terms of reduced pressure for catch-up. Some gap remained, however, possibly because the employment and profit situation remained relatively bright in Sector B. Table 4.7 summarizes a special tabulation of data assembled for the Pay Board concerning major contracts expiring in 1973. The average annual wage rate increase provided by those contracts, including cost-of-living escalator adjustments, was 8.9 percent outside construction and 9.1 percent including construction. Thus, workers under these contracts had received significant real wage gains.* This reduction in catch-up pressure appears to have been a major factor in the decision to move to Phase III. It was felt that the major contracts could be handled through less formal procedures than the Phase II mechanism provided and that the resulting wage increases would set the pattern for other settlements.[17] In addition, deferred adjustments were scheduled to be more moderate in 1973 than in 1972.†

The reduction in catch-up pressure in the union sector obviously was helpful in dealing with the key bargaining settlements during Phases III and IV, although of course catch-up was not entirely absent from these key bargains, since some groups had received below-average adjustments under their contracts. Both the apparel and electrical equipment contracts, covering 60,000 and 75,000 workers respectively, appear to have averaged less than 7 percent per annum under their expiring contracts. On the other hand, the major contracts expiring in transportation, including trucking (400,000 workers), railroads (500,000 workers), and longshoring (15,000 workers) appear to have provided affected workers with over 9 percent per annum.

Because of the reduction in the effective comprehensiveness of Phase III and IV wage controls, and the change in the structure of the controls, it was possible to devote attention to key bargaining situations prior to the conclusion of negotiations. Labor returned to the controls mechanism through the device of an advisory committee, shielded from the unpleasant Phase II task of having to vote on specific contracts and policies. Efforts were made to start negotiations early and to avoid intergroup competition. For example, the railroad agreement was reached early in 1973 and did not require the usual emergency-dispute intervention that had characterized that industry in the past. The Chicago truckdriver locals were persuaded to follow the Teamsters' Master Freight Agreement rather than leapfrog it and provoke a

---

*The average contract duration was close to three years (33 months). During 1970-73 the consumer price index rose at an annual rate of 4.6 percent. Thus, on average, a real gain of over 4 percent per year had been experienced. Comparable data for all of 1972 are not available, but for the last half of 1972 the average annual increase experienced by nonconstruction workers under major expiring contracts was 7.6 percent, according to Pay Board staff paper OCE-99, November 22, 1972.

†The Bureau of Labor Statistics estimated that the average deferred adjustment during 1972 would have been 7.1 percent including escalators on the assumption of a 3 percent increase in the consumer price index. Under the same assumption, deferred adjustments would have come to 5.9 percent in 1973. However, the fact that the actual price increase far exceeded 3 percent in 1973 means that the 1973 deferred increases were closer than anticipated to the 1972 increases.

renegotiation, as had occurred during the two previous negotiations. A 1973 agreement was reached in the steel industry providing for a no-strike dispute settlement mechanism when the existing contract would expire in 1974.

During Phase II, expectations of continued inflation on the part of labor negotiators appeared to diminish. The incidence of escalator clauses tended to drop off during 1972, a sign that fears of future infla-tion were diminishing.* The drop off in escalators was notable because the costing rules of the Pay Board actually gave incentive to the use of such devices.† During 1973 the proportion of workers covered by esca-lators under major contracts remained at about the 1972 level. However, the industry composition of negotiations meant that a greater proportion of the workers negotiating were covered by escalators.

While the Phase III and IV wage controls were able to make use of the calming of expectations that had occurred during Phase II, the reality of a rapid rate of inflation in 1973 began to rekindle pressure to protect the real value of wage gains. During the first half of 1973 consumer prices rose at an annual rate of 8. 2 percent; the second half of the year saw a 9. 4 percent annual rate. The fact that the price problems were centered in food, the later petroleum, may have suggested to some negotiators that the problems were temporary, but a trend toward the creative use of escalator clauses began to develop.

A number of escalator formulas were sweetened by providing more money for a given price rise or by removing caps on the amount the escalator could add to the basic wage. The auto contracts in the later part of 1973 were negotiated to provide the Cost of Living Council with a moderate-sounding "3 percent plus 12 cents," but the escalator clause appeared to provide a substantially greater increase during 1973

---

*Outside the construction industry (in which escalators are rare) 54. 5 percent of workers covered by new major contracts were covered by escalators in 1971. The proportion fell to 25. 8 percent in 1972 and 49. 7 percent in 1973. These figures reflect in part the industry compo-sition of expiring contracts. In the Bureau of Labor Statistics files the propor-tion of all workers under major contracts with escalators declined gradually from a peak of 41 percent at the beginning of 1972 to 38 percent at the beginning of 1974. See George Ruben, "Major Collective Bargaining Development—A Quarter-Century Review," Current Wage Developments 26 (February 1974), p. 45.

†The Pay Board permitted time-weighting of escalator adjustments. This meant that the adjustment was weighted by the proportion of the control year during which it was effective. An incentive was created to put escalator adjustments in effect late in the year. Such adjustments would not count much against the allowable 5. 5 percent, but would raise the base wage for calculating the next year's 5. 5 percent.

and in later years. This was combined with significant fringe improvements. One of the major concessions by management was a plan to place restrictions on the assignment of involuntary overtime. Such a provision, thought to be potentially expensive, would not show up with normal Stabilization Program costing techniques. In short, the auto agreements may mark the point at which the 1973 price inflation first affected a major negotiation. A few months after the auto agreements, the steelworkers provided restricted escalator protection to pensions in the aluminum industry, an innovation for a major contract.

The need of the COLC to maintain a moderate appearance in major negotiations in late 1973 and early 1974 stemmed from the Administration's desire to eliminate most economic controls. Given the rate of inflation that had accompanied these negotiations, major challenges to the resulting contracts would not have been feasible. The needs of the Cost of Living Council, which were rekindled inflationary expectations for the short term and uncertainty about the long term, combined to enhance the emphasis on escalator adjustments. In some respects escalators themselves can be considered inflationary, since they speed up the reaction time between price and wage increases. In the words of President Johnson, "Arrangements which automatically tie wage rates to changes in consumer prices will contribute to inflation."[18] On the other hand, successes in slowing price inflation will have a more immediate effect on wages where escalators are in use. Thus, whether the incentive given to escalators was a Good Thing or a Bad Thing should be determined by economic developments during the post-Phase IV period.

During Phase II, despite the incentives given to expanding qualified fringe benefits at the behest of Congress, there did not seem to be a fringe boom. By some measures, in fact, fringe activity was below earlier rates.[19] At this writing, only preliminary data are available of fringe activity in 1973. However, the appendix to this chapter suggests that fringes formed a bigger part of the compensation increase in 1973 than in 1972. This could be a reflection of the pressure from the Cost of Living Council for moderate-appearing contracts. Fringe increases tend to catch the public eye less than wage rate increases. A move toward fringes could also reflect the diminished catch-up pressure in 1973, which may have shown up as a reduced demand for cash wages relative to benefits.

The experience in the selective control areas added in Phase III is difficult to evaluate for lack of data. Average hourly earnings in hospitals continued to rise relatively slowly during 1973, 4.8 percent on a December-to-December basis. The health sector had not shown itself to be a particular problem on the wage side prior to Phase III. Concern about the health sector appeared to come mainly from the price side, and wage controls were included largely for symmetry. Earnings increases in retail food and food manufacturing during 1973 were roughly in line with those in other industries, but somewhat ahead of the 1972 rates. In food manufacturing this probably reflects the major contract expirations that occurred in 1973 in meat packing and canning. Food manufacturing wages were kept under selective control, largely due to the general anxiety over food price developments.

Retail food was also subject to selective controls partly for price symmetry reasons, but also because of pressure in union settlements uncovered during Phase II. An effort was made by the Cost of Living Council to set up a wage controls mechanism in retail food that was modeled after the procedures used in construction. It is not clear, however, that the retail food wage problem was based on the craft-oriented leap-frogging patterns that occurred in construction. In any case the lack of union sector wage data in retail food and the failure of the Food Wage and Salary Committee to maintain public records make it difficult to come to any conclusions.

During Phases III and IV, controls in construction appeared to continue the calming influence that had developed earlier. Unlike those of the other selective control sectors, wages in construction had been under an ongoing system for some time, and hence no start-up costs were incurred by construction wage controls in Phase III.

BYPRODUCTS OF WAGE CONTROLS

I have noted earlier that the product market seems to be more prone to economic distortion under controls than the labor market. The prominent examples of distortions that occurred during Phase I through IV are all product shortages, that is, the beef, gasoline, paper, lumber, and cement problems that occurred at various times under controls. There do not appear to have been any widespread labor shortages.

During Phase II the staff of the Pay Board made a determined hunt for occupational labor shortages but was unable to find any. [20] Despite the fact that it was difficult to obtain an exception based on a labor shortage during Phase II, the labor market was not especially tight at that time. The unemployment rate averaged 5.6 percent in 1972. By 1973 the labor market tightened, and unemployment fell to 4.9 percent. However, the controls program was also relaxed in 1973. The acceleration in wages in the nonunion sector might have meant a collision with the 5.5 percent standard, had the old framework been continued. Nonunion employers were relatively free to adjust wages to meet market conditions after Phase II. Since flexibility was allowed at the competitive end of the labor market where shortages were more prone to occur, it is not surprising that controls-related recruitment problems continued to be notable for their absence.

Manufacturing quit rates can be explained on an annual basis (1951-73) by time, the ratio of real goods (G) output to logarithmic trend, and dummies for 1972 (D72) and for 1973 (D73). The resulting regression with t statistics in parentheses was:

$$\text{Quit} = -9.21 + .003 \text{ Time} + 11.14G + .08D72 + .15D73$$
$$(-8.45) \quad (.34) \qquad (10.40) \quad (.29) \qquad (.57)$$
$$R^2 = .83 \quad D\text{-}W = .7737 \quad SE = .24$$

Source: Compiled by the author.

Labor shortages should be reflected in above-normal quit rates, but no significant deviations appear in 1972 or 1973. Similar results obtain if autoregressive corrections are made.

Although economic distortions in the labor market were a rarity, it is still possible that disruptions in the industrial relations system were created. There have been claims that controls stimulated unionization, presumably because above-guideline increases in major union settlements received publicity. [21] The most comprehensive data on unionization come from the results of union certification elections conducted by the National Labor Relations Board. The union win rate rose slightly during Phase II, relative to fiscal 1971. However, the various win rates shown in Table 4.8 do not seem out of line with earlier years, particularly when the gradual downward trend in the figures is considered. It would be interesting to speculate whether the 1973 drop in Teamster wins in the "all election" category, which includes election contests between the Teamsters and other unions, reflects the loss of special status by that union after Phase II. After the labor walkout in March 1972, the Teamsters were the only labor "insiders" in the Stabilization Program until Phase III. However, there is insufficient information to make any judgment on this matter.

Strikes aimed against the program were a rarity. Only a handful of such instances occurred. The number of stoppages in 1972 (5,010) and 1973 (5,600) was lower than the postwar peak of 1969-70, but high by general postwar standards. On the other hand, the proportion of working time lost to stoppages (15 percent in 1972 and 14 percent in 1973) was low, but not record breaking, relative to the general postwar level.

It was feared by some that collective bargaining would erode under controls. Employers might decide it was to their advantage to accept any union demands put forth, in hopes that the wage authorities would step in and enforce a rollback. Such tactics could contribute to a reduction in strike activity. However, the only industry in Phase II where this tendency seemed to appear was in retail foodstores. The relatively high requests coming to the Pay Board in retail food (10.7 percent for new union contracts in Categories I and II) contributed to the decision to keep the industry under selective controls after Phase II. Conceivably this decision might have aggravated the problem of erosion.

TABLE 4. 8

Union Representation Elections

Fiscal Year	Union Wins as Percent of Elections		Teamster Wins as Percent of Elections Involving Teamsters	
	One-Union Elections	All Elections	One-Union Elections	All Elections
1964	54	57	54	57
1965	57	60	55	60
1966	58	61	57	61
1967	56	59	58	61
1968	54	57	55	59
1969	51	55	51	55
1970	52	55	52	56
1971	50	53	49	53
December 1971 to December 1972	52	53	52	55
January 1973 to December 1973	50	52	50	49

Source: National Labor Relations Board, Election Report, various issues.

The one area of collective bargaining in which the industrial relations system did appear to suffer a clear distortion was contract duration. One of the special features of the U. S. industrial relations
system has been the development of multi-year contracts, which provide
prolonged periods of labor peace. Table 4. 9 shows that in 1971, when
controls were placed on construction, the proportion of one-year contracts rose from 7 percent to 63 percent, according to a survey of the
Bureau of National Affairs, Inc. (Construction controls came early in
that year.) A peak of 84 percent was reached in 1972. A similar
effect, although much less pronounced, was noticeable in the nonconstruction sector of the reduced comprehensiveness of wage controls. [22]
These figures are influenced by the industry composition of negotiations.
It should also be noted that industries usually characterized by short
contracts will tend to be over-represented in the samples, since expirations are more likely to occur in such industries in any given year.
    The contract shortening phenomenon probably reflects the effect of
uncertainty engendered by controls on the parties to union agreements.

Apparently it was felt that the best thing to do in the face of uncertainty about how long wage controls would endure was to negotiate short contracts. These would allow renegotiations in the near future, should controls be ended.

SUMMARY

Wages were the heart of the Economic Stabilization Program begun in 1971. Price controls were based on markups and pass-throughs, so that without wage stability, price stability could not be achieved. Wage controls were not designed to push wage increases below "normal" with respect to other economic conditions, but instead to bring the catch-up pressure that had developed in the union sector to an orderly end. It is not clear that the process would not have occurred in the absence of controls, but there was concern that the momentum built up during the catch-up stage could continue beyond the point at which catch-up had been achieved. It does seem that the collective bargaining sector calmed down under controls.

From the point of view of administration, it appears from hindsight that the comprehensiveness of the Phase II wage controls was excessive, particularly in relation to the staff available to operate them. There was something to be said, however, for starting with a fairly expansive program and then narrowing it to key settlements and problem sectors. The experience in construction indicates that selective controls have their use in dealing with sectoral difficulties. There is little evidence to show whether or not the construction model was of much use in food and health, the two industries singled out for selective wage controls after Phase II ended.

APPENDIX

Because of the relatively short periods involved and the various factors that influence the common measures of wage change, it is difficult to say precisely what the underlying rate of wage change actually was during the different stages of controls. Table 4.10 shows that on a December-to-December basis, the hourly earnings index rose by 6.3 percent during 1972; the 1973 rate was 6.7 percent. This index covers nonsupervisory workers in the private nonfarm sector and is corrected for interindustry employment shift and overtime in manufacturing. It is therefore as close to an aggregate wage rate index as American data can provide. However, the omission of fringes and supervisory employees is a serious deficiency.

TABLE 4.9

Durations of New Contracts
(in percent)

	One Year	Two Years	Three Years	Four Years or More
Nonconstruction				
1970	8	38	53	1
1971	6	35	58	1
1972	15	34	51	0
1973	10	36	54	0
Construction				
1970	7	43	48	2
1971	63	24	13	0
1972	84	12	4	0
1973	78	18	4	0

Note: Contracts surveyed numbered 2,819 in 1970; 3,042 in 1971; 2,790 in 1972; and 4,405 in 1973.

Source: Bureau of National Affairs, Daily Labor Report, various issues.

Fringes and supervisory workers are included in the index of compensation per manhour, but this index is available only quarterly and is not corrected for interindustry shift and overtime. Measuring 1972 on a quarterly basis raises the 1972 wage increase rate by .2 percent because of the shift in the timing of increases (bulge) caused by the end of the Phase I freeze in November 1971. Another .2 percent was added by interindustry shift and overtime during 1972 and another .3 percent during 1973. When these earnings changes are scaled down proportionate to the percentage of total compensation accounted for by earnings, the result is 6 percent in 1972 and 6.2 percent in 1973. The deviations among these figures and movements in compensation per manhour are presumably accounted for by fringe adjustments, changes in Social Security taxes, and the addition of supervisory workers. Since Social Security increases added about .7 percent to total compensation in 1972 and about .8 percent in 1973, the remaining .4 percent and 1 percent in 1972 and 1973 are the result of including fringe benefits and supervisors.

These data (Table 4.10) provide at best rough estimates of underlying compensation changes. A crude estimate of private wage and fringe adjustments can be made by adding Lines 6 and 8 and subtracting Lines 2 and 3.

TABLE 4.10

Changes in Compensation Indexes
for Private, Nonfarm Sector
(in percent)

	From End of 1971 to End of 1972	From End of 1972 to End of 1973
1. Hourly earnings index, December-to-December basis	6.3	6.7
2. Effect of including post-Phase-I bulge through use of quarterly data	0.2	not applicable
3. Hourly earnings index, fourth-quarter-to-fourth-quarter basis.	6.5	6.7
4. Effect of interindustry shift and change in manufacturing overtime.	0.2	0.3
5. Average hourly earnings, fourth-quarter-to-fourth-quarter basis	6.7	7.0
6. Average hourly earnings on base of total compensation	6.0	6.2
7. Effect of Social Security tax increases	0.7	0.8
8. Effect of fringe benefits, for supervisors and certain other nonpayroll employees	0.4	1.1
9. Compensation per manhour, fourth-quarter-to-fourth-quarter basis	7.1	8.1

Source: Lines 1, 3, 5, and 9 are from Current Wage Developments; Line 2 is the difference between Line 3 and Line 1; Line 4 is the difference between Line 5 and Line 3; Line 8 is the difference between Line 9 and Line 6 less Line 7; Line 6 is Line 5 multiplied by the proportion of compensation represented by wages and salaries, from Survey of Current Business, July 1973, Table 6, p. 41; Line 7, for 1972, is the employer's share of social insurance per full-time equivalent employee tabulated from Survey of Current Business, July 1973, Table 1.10, p. 21, and Table 6.4, p. 42; this figure was taken as a percentage of 1971 compensation (including fringes) per full-time equivalent employee in the private sector; Line 6 estimate for 1973 is based on Pay Board staff paper OCE-112, December 20, 1972.

This suggests an underlying change, excluding bulge, shift, overtime, and Social Security taxes of about 6 percent in 1972 and about 7 percent in 1973. On the other hand, economic theory suggests that the incidence of the Social Security tax should fall on labor. Thus, Social Security tax increases may simply have substituted for other forms of compensation. [23] In that case, Line 7 should be added to the previous estimates, suggesting underlying changes of 6.7 percent in 1972 and 7.8 percent in 1973. It is likely, however, that the complete absorption did not take place. For example, workers under existing contracts could not easily be made to absorb the increases. Thus the probable underlying rates of wage and fringe adjustments during 1972 and 1973 were in the lower 6 percent and the lower 7 percent ranges respectively.

NOTES

1. A thorough exposition of this approach appears in Don Patinkin, Money, Interest, and Prices 2nd ed., (New York: Harper & Row, 1965).

2. Arthur M. Ross, Trade Union Wage Policy (Berkeley: University of California Press, 1948).

3. This point is discussed in Milton Friedman, "What Price Guideposts?" in George P. Shultz and Robert Z. Aliber, Guidelines: Informal Controls and the Market Place (Chicago: University of Chicago Press, 1966), p. 21.

4. See Daniel J. B. Mitchell, "Union Wage Policies: The Ross-Dunlop Debate Reopened," Industrial Relations 11 (February 1972), pp. 46-61.

5. The emphasis on changing inflationary expectations was quite clear from Administration statements. See the statement by Herbert Stein, Chairman of the Council of Economic Advisors in U.S. Joint Economic Committee, Review of Phase II of the New Economic Program, 92nd cong., 2nd sess. (Washington, D.C.: Government Printing Office, 1972), pp. 7-17. For a conceptual treatment of the expectations approach to controls, see Daniel J. B. Mitchell, "A Simplified Approach to Incomes Policy," Industrial and Labor Relations Review, 22 (July 1969), pp. 512-27.

6. Excerpted from U.S. Joint Economic Committee, Review of Phase II of the New Economic Program, 92nd cong., 2nd sess. (Washington, D.C.: Government Printing Office, 1972), p. 254.

7. Data obtained by the author from the Internal Revenue Service.

8. Ibid.

9. U.S. Senate Committee on Banking, Housing and Urban Affairs, Subcommittee on Production and Stabilization, "Statement of Dr. John T. Dunlop," 93rd cong., 2nd sess., February 6, 1974 (Washington, D.C.: Government Printing Office, 1974), Appendix O.

10. Ibid., Appendix J.
11. George L. Perry, "Wages and the Guideposts," American Economic Review 57 (September 1967), pp. 897-904. Comments appear in the American Economic Review 59: (June 1969), pp. 351-370. Application of the residual technique to the Economic Stabilization Program can be found in Robert J. Gordon, "The Response of Wages and Prices to the First Two Years of Controls," Brookings Papers on Economic Activity, no. 3 (1973), pp. 765-78; Robert J. Gordon, "Wage-Price Controls and the Shifting Phillips Curve," Brookings Papers on Economic Activity, no. 2 (1972), pp. 385-421; Robert F. Lanzillotti and Blaine Roberts, "An Assessment of the U.S. Experiment with an Incomes Policy," paper presented at the Tulane Conference on Incomes Policies, April 1973 (unpublished). A discussion of the results of these and other efforts to evaluate the Economic Stabilization Program can be found in U.S. Senate Committee on Banking, Housing and Urban Affairs, op. cit., Appendix N. An example of the residual technique applied to a foreign controls program can be found in Daniel J. B. Mitchell, "Incomes Policy and the Labor Market in France," Industrial and Labor Relations Review 25 (April 1972), pp. 315-35.
12. John Sheahan, The Wage-Price Guideposts (Washington, D.C.: the Brookings Institution, 1967), p. 12.
13. U.S. President, Economic Report of the President (Washington, D.C.: Government Printing Office, 1973), pp. 52-53, 62.
14. Discussion of these data in more detail can be found in Daniel J. B. Mitchell, "Phase II Wage Controls" Industrial and Labor Relations Review 27 (April 1974, pp. 351-75.
15. Ibid., pp. 370-72.
16. Ibid., p. 372, especially Footnote 37.
17. See Marvin Kosters, Kenneth Fedor, and Albert Eckstein, "Collective Bargaining Settlements and the Wage Structure," Labor Law Journal 24 (August 1973), pp. 517-25. This article was originally an internal staff paper written during Phase II at the Cost of Living Council.
18. U.S. President, Economic Report of the President (Washington, D.C.: Government Printing Office, 1967), p. 129.
19. Mitchell, "Phase II Wage Controls," op. cit., pp. 355-57.
20. Pay Board staff paper OCE-103, November 28, 1972.
21. National Association of Manufacturers, Industry Survey on Wage and Price Controls (Washington, D.C.: The Association, 1974), p. 34.
22. Daily Labor Report, various issues.
23. John A. Brittain, "The Incidence of Social Security Payroll Taxes," American Economic Review 56 (March 1971), pp. 110-25.

5

TREATMENT OF ESCALATORS
UNDER WAGE AND PRICE
CONTROLS

Jerome M. Staller
Loren M. Solnick

Changes in living costs have long been an integral factor in determining wage changes. Through much of the first half of this century the
relationship between rising living costs and wage increases was somewhat gratuitous, but since 1948 collective bargaining agreements have
made this relationship explicit. This has been accomplished through
the use of cost of living escalator adjustment provisions (COLAs).
Escalator clauses specify in advance the relationship between wage
changes and price changes.

Although all escalator provisions specify a functional relationship
between changes in the Consumer Price Index (CPI) and the wage rates
of workers, there are numerous variations in the form of the function.
Escalator clauses are generally so phrased that a given index point
increase of the CPI yields a specified cents-per-hour increase in
wages; for example a . 3 point increase in the CPI yeilds a wage hike
of 1 cent per hour. Less typical are those formulations that relate an
absolute increase in wages to a percentage change in the CPI or those
that provide for a percentage change in wages corresponding exactly
to the percentage change in prices.

During inflationary periods, considerable absorption of rising
living costs tends to occur between the relatively infrequent renegotiations of wage scales. Wage adjustments that occur as the result of
contract reopeners or the negotiation of new contracts are accomplished
with considerable uncertainty and delay, which cost-of-living escalators
are designed to reduce. [1]

The existence of escalator provisions in many collective bargaining
agreements ensures that as long as prices advance, wages will also
continue to rise. Since this automatically adds to labor costs, it tends
to exacerbate inflation. This circular relationship—price change→wage
change→price change—has created a major issue that has faced wage
and price controllers in the recent as well as past control periods. The
question is, "How should cost of living wage increases be treated?"

THE PROBLEM CONFRONTING CONTROLLERS

There are three major considerations, oftentimes in conflict, confronting wage controllers when they attempt to determine the appropriate policy for treating cost of living escalators.

1. Stabilization: Restriction of the size of wage and fringe benefit increases to limit the pressure on prices.

2. Maintenance of real income: Allowing wages to rise as fast as prices to maintain real earnings.

3. Equal treatment: Balancing different types of contract provisions for the revision of wage scales.

The remainder of this chapter is concerned with the efforts made to strike a balance among these considerations during the various stabilization periods.

THE NATIONAL WAR LABOR BOARD (1941-46)

The National War Labor Board placed major emphasis on the stabilization consideration. A conscious effort was made by the board to break the tie between the general wage level and the cost of living. The War Labor Board took the position that support of the war effort involved the transfer of resources from domestic uses to military uses.[2] With a large proportion of the nation's total output being devoted to national defense, it was inevitable that real incomes would decline. Not to recognize this fact would disguise the real costs of the war and result in an inflationary spiral as the public sector competed with the private sector for the limited goods and services the nation could produce.

Escalator clauses in 1942 were limited almost entirely to the shipbuilding industry.[3] Since they were not in wide use, they did not present problems of the magnitude of those faced by wage controllers in subsequent periods. The escalator clauses in the shipbuilding industry were adopted in 1941. Under four separate zone agreements, they covered all the major shipyards in the United States. Adjustments were to be made every six months, based on changes in the Bureau of Labor Statistics Cost of Living Index (now the Consumer Price Index). At the request of the President, management and labor held the National Shipbuilding Conference in May 1942. As a result of this conference, there was an agreement to delete the escalator provision from the contracts.[4]

Subsequent to this agreement the National War Labor Board issued General Order 22, which prohibited the operation of the relatively few existing escalator clauses in collective bargaining agreements beyond the limit set by the "Little Steel" formula, which permitted an increase

in straight-time hourly earnings of 15 percent over the January 1941
levels. This formulation, which covered all contracts including shipbuilding, was designed to restore wage relationships along the lines
prevailing prior to the start of the war. The 15 percent figure was
derived from the change in the cost of living index over the period
January 1941 to May 1942. Subsequent changes in the cost of living,
though substantial, were not incorporated into the formula. The elimi-
nation of the shipbuilding escalator agreements clearly indicated that
the board was more concerned with stabilization than with the maintenance of real wages. By following this course, the board was also able
to avoid the equal treatment issue.

THE WAGE STABILIZATION PROGRAM (1950-53)

By 1951, when the Wage Stabilization Board was established, there
had been a significant increase in the popularity and acceptance of
escalators; contracts with escalators covered over 3 million workers.
The approach and policies of the Wage Stabilization Board were affected
not only by the number of contracts that had escalators but also by the
nature of the mobilization effort, since there was a much smaller military buildup during the Korean conflict than during World War II.
The Wage Stabilization Board faced two distinct collective bargaining
patterns for general wage adjustments, annual across-the-board increases
and long-term escalator provisions. Each of these patterns posed its
own special set of difficulties. The reconciliation of these differences
in a single set of policies in a manner that retained equity was a major
consideration of the wage controllers. [5]
In 1951, the predominant pattern for adjusting general wage levels
consisted of annual across-the-board increases negotiated in one-year
contracts. The magnitude of these adjustments tended to increase
during inflationary periods and spread in an irregular but rapid manner
throughout the economy.
The 1948 Auto Workers-General Motors collective bargaining agreement established the second pattern. Multi-year contracts that provided
for an annual improvement factor (productivity increase) and a cost of
living escalator were negotiated. The existence of escalator provisions
covering over 3 million workers forced the Wage Stabilization Board to
pay more attention to the real wage concern and consequently to equal
treatment.
As might be expected, the management and labor representatives
to the Wage Stabilization Board did not always agree on the appropriate
policy toward cost-of-living wage increases. The typical management
position is given in the following quote from a board member representing
the Chamber of Commerce:

We recognize that under normal peacetime conditions a cost
of living escalator clause in a wage contract may be proper.
But, in a defense economy, we condemn the use of the
escalator principle in wage contracts and in the government's
wage stabilization program. In a defense economy, such a
provision is a dangerous fraud because it promises something
that cannot be delivered and promotes inflation. [6]

Labor's position was indicated by the following statement made
before the board on behalf of the United Labor Policy Committee:

1. All groups of workers should be allowed wage adjustments
to compensate for increases in the cost of living regardless of
whether these adjustments are secured through existing contract
provisions, or through other means. The desires and practices
of the groups immediately concerned should determine the method.
2. Contractual provisions adjusting wages to the Consumer
Price Index should be approved where the collective bargaining
parties have chosen to negotiate such provisions.
3. There should be no limitation on wage adjustments to compensate for living cost increases. [7]

The issues of general wage policy and cost of living escalation
preoccupied the Wage Stabilization Board for over six months. There
were numerous proposals and counterproposals put forth to deal with
these two major issues; out of this debate, two general regulations
that governed board policy in these areas were established. General
Wage Regulation 6 permitted general increases in wage and salary
levels up to 10 percent over the wage and salary levels in effect on
January 15, 1950. General Wage Regulation 8 permitted the operation
of cost-of-living provisions in collective bargaining agreements and
written wage and salary plans that were based on an acceptable cost-
of-living index. In the absence of a formal plan, General Wage Regulation 8 permitted semiannual cost-of-living increases based on an
acceptable index to restore the loss in the real value of wages from
January 25, 1951, to the date of the increase. [8]

In essence GWR 6 was a catch-up formula that was designed to
allow labor to make up any loss in real wages over the January 1950
to January 1951 period. GWR 8 established the fact that the board
recognized that maintenance of real wages was a primary consideration.
As it was originally issued in March 1951, GWR 8 applied only to contracts having cost-of-living escalator provisions and to written wage
and salary plans in effect prior to January 1951. Acceptance of the
principle that wages should be adjusted to changes in the cost of living

and equity considerations brought about the more general phrasing that
was eventually adopted. *

While the Wage Stabilization Board emphasized real wage and equity
considerations, it did not totally ignore the stabilization concern. It
was hoped that, by holding real wages relatively constant rather than
permitting them to rise, the stabilization goal would be achieved.

THE PAY BOARD AND THE COST OF LIVING COUNCIL
(NOVEMBER 1971 TO APRIL 1974)

The economic and political environment in which the Pay Board
operated was more like the environment during the Korean conflict than
that of World War II. Both the Wage Stabilization Board and the Pay
Board came into existence while the country was in a state of partial
mobilization, and in both instances the economy was in the midst of
a recovery from a small recession and prices were rising at levels
deemed unsatisfactory.

Between June 1950 and January 1951 the CPI rose 6.6 percent,
whereas from January 1971, to July 1971 the CPI rose 2.2 percent. Unemployment was running well over 5 percent prior to the 1971-74 controls
period, while the rate was in the vicinity of 6 percent in 1950. Of
more direct concern to wage policy formulation was the similarity of
the collective bargaining emvironment during the two periods. In each
case there were a significant number of workers who were receiving
deferred wage increases under collective bargaining agreements. There
were over 4 million workers covered by cost-of-living escalator provisions in 1971. Thus, as had the Wage Stabilization Board, the Pay
Board was forced to address the issues of real earnings and equal treatment in addition to the problem of stabilization.

By the 1970s it was commonplace to view wage increases as con-
sisting of the two components embodied in the 1948 agreement between
GM and the Auto Workers: productivity and cost of living. The goal of
the controls program was to reduce the annual rate of inflation to between
2 and 3 percent. The nation's long-run productivity gains had averaged
about 3 percent per year and were expected to continue at that rate; thus, pay
increases had to be limited to an average of between 5 and 6 percent. [9]

---

*As originally promulgated, GWR 8 operating in conjunction with
GWR 6 would have created a number of inequitable situations (1) between
contracts with escalators negotiated prior to January 1951 and those
negotiated after January 1951; (2) between contracts with escalators
prior to January 1951 and those with escalators negotiated after January
1951; and (3) in contracts on policies in practice having escalators prior
to January 1951 and in nonunion situations without any such practices.

The Pay Board took the position that much of the current inflation was of the cost-push variety and that if the level of wage increases could be limited to 6 percent, subsequent price increases would only reflect the higher labor costs associated with inflation. However, until the objective of a 2 to 3 percent inflation rate was achieved, the board had to face the very real problem that wage increases, especially those in collective bargaining agreements calling for deferred wage increases, were likely to exceed the stated 5.5 percent standard.

Two basic regulations were promulgated to deal with the problem. The first regulation provided a 7 percent standard for pay increases in contracts negotiated prior to the freeze date of August 14, 1971. The second regulation allowed for cost-of-living escalator increases to be time weighted. Time weighting provided that wage increases obtained through escalators could be counted only in proportion to the time they were in effect during a control year. For example, an escalator increase that raised base compensation by 1 percent but was payable halfway through a control year counted only as a .5 percent increase.

The 7 percent standard was designed to appease labor's concern about being penalized retroactively and also to recognize that price increases could not initially be reduced to the desired rate. By setting this higher limit on deferred increases, the board hoped to ensure that the real wages of the covered workers would not be eroded.

Time weighting provided a method of avoiding the escalator issue. The simple mathematics of the situation made it highly unlikely that contracts containing escalators would be subject to a cutback. Contracts having escalators usually provide a 3 to 4 percent general increase, ostensibly to cover increased productivity, in addition to the escalator. Assuming that price increases occur evenly throughout the year and that escalators generally add 1 percent to wages for each 1 percent increase in prices, [10] then prices would have had to rise at more than 6 percent per year before the 7 percent standards would be exceeded.

The administrative machinery, whether by accident or by design, also resulted in favorable treatment for contracts containing an escalator. The Pay Board approved the pay increases contained in contracts at the beginning of a contract year. If a contract contained an escalator the parties were asked to estimate the time-weighted value of such increases at the beginning of the contract year along with the value of other increases. This required an assumption regarding future price increases by the parties. The usual assumption was 2.5 percent, the program goal. Although the parties were supposed to notify the Pay Board if actual cost-of-living increases exceeded the estimate, the appropriate forms were significant by their absence at the Pay Board. It is not surprising, then, that during the entire course of Phase II no deferred increase containing an escalator was cut back. Although there were some first-year increases in contracts that contained escalator clauses that were trimmed back; since the escalators did not come into play until the second contract year one could not deem this a cutback related to escalators. Thus, while in principle escalated contracts and nonescalated contracts were subject to the same standards, in practice they were not.

During Phases III and IV of the economic controls program the standards established by the Pay Board were retained, but in practice there was no set standard. Through the offices of the Director of the Cost of Living Council, John Dunlop, each situation was evaluated with regard to a number of unspecified criteria. One must assume, given the level of both new and deferred increases during Phase III and IV, that maintenance of the real wage, whether through escalators or other means, was a primary consideration. During this period also, there is no record of an escalator wage increase having been reduced.

The Pay Board's policies clearly did not treat all wage increases equally. Available data permit at least a cursory evaluation of the impact of the policies of the Pay Board (and subsequently the Cost of Living Council's) on the wage structure and on real earnings. The Bureau of Labor Statistics has tabulated the actual realized wage gains for workers covered by major collective bargaining agreements expiring in 1974. These tabulations include all regularly scheduled increases, initial and deferred, as well as actual escalator increases. Table 5.1 presents data on the average annual rate of wage change among major three-year contracts expiring in 1974. These contracts were negotiated in 1971 and thus span the period of wage and price controls.

Several qualifications with respect to the data are in order before examining the figures presented. First, some of the contracts were negotiated prior to August 1971 and therefore were permitted larger wage increases than contracts negotiated after the controls were in effect. However, the proportion of the contracts negotiated before August that contained escalators is not known, and therefore the direction of any possible bias is also unknown. Second, the escalator increases were tabulated through October 1973 only. Since there were additional escalator increases between October 1973 and April 1974, the data tend to understate the differences in the wage gains of workers covered by escalators and those not covered. Third, the wage experience of workers negotiating shorter-term contracts is not included in these data.

The figures in Table 5.1 suggest that over a time period that roughly corresponds to the period of controls the workers covered by contracts with escalators realized wage gains that averaged almost 2 percent more per year than the wage gains of workers whose contracts did not contain an escalator provision. Over the life of the contracts (and during the control period) these figures imply about a 6 percent gain by workers covered by escalators.

Data for major two-year contracts expiring in 1974 were also analyzed. These contracts fall completely within the control period because they were negotiated in 1972. As above, escalator increases

TABLE 5.1

Average Annual Rates of Wage Increase Over the
Lives of Major Three-Year Contracts Expiring in 1974
(in percent)

	Type of Contract	
	With Escalators	Without Escalators
All Industries	9.8	8.0
Manufacturing	9.9	6.7
Nonmanufacturing (excluding construction)	9.5	8.9

Source: Office of Wages and Industrial Relations, Bureau of Labor
Statistics, unpublished memo.

after October 1973 were not included in the data. These data reveal
that workers whose contracts contained escalator clauses realized
average annual wage increases over the life of the contract of 8 percent,
compared with 6.6 percent for workers not covered by escalators. Lack
of two-year escalator agreements outside of the manufacturing sector
precludes a more detailed breakdown of the data. These figures imply
about a 3 percent gain for workers with escalators during the 1972-74
period. The data clearly suggest that the wage regulations of the 1971-
74 controls (specifically the time weighting of wage increases obtained
through escalators) permitted the wages of workers covered by escalators
to rise more rapidly than the wages of workers not covered by escalators.

The effect of the controls program on real earnings can be estimated.
Among the many series published by the Bureau of Labor Statistics, the
Average Hourly Earnings Index for the private, nonfarm sector may best
reflect the movement of wages. This index is adjusted for overtime hours
in manufacturing and for interindustry shifts in employment. Table 5.2
presents the Average Hourly Earnings Index for major sectors of the
economy for August 1971 and for April 1974. The third column shows
the latter figures adjusted for the increase in the CPI over the period.
Except in the construction industry, real average hourly earnings
(adjusted) appear to have been almost unchanged over the control period.
The drop in real average hourly earnings for the construction industry
undoubtedly reflects the special concern that was shown about rising
wages in that industry.[*]

---

[*]The Construction Industry Stabilization Committee, for example,
predates the Economic Stabilization Programs.

TABLE 5. 2

Average Hourly Earnings Index for
Private, Nonfarm Sector, August 1971 and April 1974
(seasonally adjusted)

	August 1974	April 1974	April 1974*
Manufacturing	128.7	151.4	128.3
Nonmanufacturing	131.5	155.8	132.0
Construction	139.5	154.6	131.0
Total	130.9	154.5	130.9

*Adjusted for the increase in the CPI from August 1971 to April 1974.
Source: Employment and Earnings, 20, no. 11 (May 1974) Table C-17
and Employment and Earnings, 17, no. 3 (September 1971) Table C-17.

SUMMARY

It appears that the 1971-74 wage controls were successful in maintaining real earnings, except in construction, but not in extending equal treatment to all contractual wage increases. The extent to which stability was achieved by the controls has been, and will continue to be, widely debated. An additional analysis here would be inappropriate. Under the controls of World War II, the real wage consideration was secondary to the concerns of stabilization and equity. On the other hand, the Wage Stabilization Board of the early 1950s emphasized the real wage issue while sacrificing in the areas of equity and stabilization.

It is clear from examination of the three periods of economic controls that the issues surrounding escalators have not changed, although the approaches or weights given to the various considerations have changed in response to changes in the underlying structure of the economy and in the political climate.

NOTES

1. For a more detailed discussion see Jerome M. Staller and Loren M. Solnick, "Effect of Escalators on Wages in Major Contracts Expiring in 1974," Monthly Labor Review 97, no. 7 (July 1974): 27-32.
2. National War Labor Board, Termination Report (Washington, D.C.: Government Printing Office, 1947), Vol. I, pp. 184-86; Vol. II, pp. 273-322.

3. Ibid., Vol. I, p. 849.

4. Ibid., Vol. I, p. 192, For a more detailed discussion see Benson Soffer, "Cost of Living Wage Policy," Industrial and Labor Relations Review 7, no. 2 (January 1954): 192-99.

5. Wage Stabilization Program 1950-1953, Wage Stabilization Board (Washington, D.C.: Govermnent Printing Office, 1953), Vol. I, p. 90.

6. Ibid., Vol. I, p. 92.

7. Ibid., Vol. I, p. 94.

8. Ibid., Vol. I, pp. 90-105 and Vol. III, p. 2.

9. See Milton Derber, "The Wage Stabilization Program in Historical Perspective," Labor Law Journal 23, no. 8 (August 1972): 457.

10. For the validity of this assumption see Audrey Freedman, "Cost of Living Clauses in Collective Bargaining," Compensation Review (Third Quarter, 1974), p. 15.

CHAPTER

6

AN ALTERNATIVE TO
WAGE AND PRICE CONTROLS
Arthur Kraft, John Kraft,
Blaine Roberts

August 15, 1971, marked the first venture of the United States into peacetime wage and price controls and the first appearance of a formal incomes policy since the Korean conflict of the early 1950s. While no one questions that some action was necessary to modify the inflation of the early 1970s, one could question whether the rigid controls of Phase I and Phase II were the appropriate action. Any such economic assessment of the controls program should be couched in a cost-benefit framework; that is, the effectiveness of Phases I and II should be compared with the costs and benefits of alternative programs on the policy frontier, such as more restrictive fiscal policy.

Our approach is to develop structural wage and price equations for the manufacturing sector, in which taxes are allowed to influence the determination of wages and prices. The taxes specifically examined are the corporate income tax, the personal income tax, and the social security tax. The presence of the tax variables in the wage and price equations will necessitate the exclusion of other variables, and thus preclude the testing of hypotheses concerning manufacturing pricing; therefore variables related to competitive supply-demand and target-rate-of-return are removed. [1] The hypothesis to be tested is whether controls or a restrictive tax policy would have resulted in a shifting of the Phillips curve, and whether a tax policy would have been more appropriate than an incomes policy.

This chapter is divided into three parts. The first section sets forth the wage and price equations. The second section is concerned with the estimation of equations and the implication for the hypothesis. The last section examines the influence of the wage-price control program on the discrete movement of wages and prices in the manufacturing sector and compares these results with those of restrictive tax policy.

WAGE AND PRICE DETERMINATION

Over the last several years many structural equation models have appeared that attempt to explain the aggregate movement of wages and prices. Some of the studies have focused on the determination of prices,[2] while others have focused on the determination of wages, [3] and still others have centered on the simultaneous determination of both wages and prices. [4] The one anomaly in the above efforts is that few have examined the influence of taxes in the determination of wages and prices. Price equations have typically excluded the corporate income tax as a possible explanatory variable in favor of such variables as unit labor costs, unit materials costs, and capital costs. The majority of the wage equations are specified as modified Phillips curves or price expectations models. The above-mentioned models provide a natural framework for testing our hypothesis.

The model presented consists of two equations for manufacturing, one explaining wages and the other explaining prices. Several features characterize this model:

1. The wage variable has been adjusted for overtime, interindustry employment shifts, and fringe benefits.

2. The model uses two price variables, a consumption price variable and a manufacturing output price variable. In the long run, output prices are transformed into consumption prices, but in the short run the movements of the two series are considerably different.

3. The model accounts for the influence of the income and social security taxes on the determination of wages.

4. The corporate income tax enters as an explanatory variable in the determination of manufacturing prices.

The Form of the Variables. Previous studies have defined the variables of the wage and price equations in levels, quarterly rates of change, and overlapping four-quarter rates of change. Each of the above specifications presents severe estimation problems. The use of levels introduces serious multicollinearity into both the wage and price equations and usually causes the simulated wage and price equations to track the actual wages and prices poorly. The one-quarter rate of change form fails to produce significant variability in the transformed series for the purposes of estimation. This is an acute problem for the manufacturing sector, but is not particularly a problem for the private nonfarm sector, where in contrast with manufacturing the fit is quite good. [5] The use of overlapping four-quarter rates of change introduces serious autocorrelation problems, however. Because of the high signal-to-noise ratio, we have chosen to use the annualized four-quarter percentage change in each variable and then correct for autocorrelation. All the rate variables are expressed in decimal as opposed to percentage form, and all lags are introduced as fixed weighted averages of past variables rather than estimated freely.

The Wage Question. Equation 1 is

$$WF_t = a + b\ PCF_t + cPCFEXP_{t-1} + d(1/U)_t + eGP_t + f\ \overline{TWF}_t.$$

The "F" suffix indicates that the variable is defined as a four-quarter rate of change. The "bar" over a variable denotes the utilization of a variable in a fixed lag form; unless stated to the contrary the fixed weight variable has the weights .4, .3, .2, and .1 for the time periods t through t - 3.

WF_t, the dependent variable of the wage equation, is the four-quarter rate of change in the fixed weight gross wage index, including fringe benefits. It is adjusted for interindustry employment shifts and overtime paid to production workers in the manufacturing sector.

Two variables in Equation 1 measure price expectations. The hypothesis is that workers form price expectations about future rates of inflation based on the past movements of prices they paid as consumers. PCF_t is the four-quarter rate of change in the GNP implicit price deflator for personal consumption expenditures. It captures the normal impact of price expectations on wages. If the coefficient is positive but less than one, this would indicate that workers perceive a minor impact on real income. However, $PCFEXP_{t-1}$ is an inflation severity variable which is zero in "normal" times, when consumer prices have risen less than 5 percent over the last two years. When inflation advances more rapidly than "normal," the workers perceive the deleterious impact that inflation has on their real incomes. As a consequence the workers form more inflationary price expectations and attempt to preserve their real incomes through bargaining for higher money wages. Thus the coefficient c on the expectations variable is expected to be positive and is counted in the determination of money wages during inflationary times.

The unemployment reciprocal $(1/U)_t$ is a proxy measure for labor-market tightness. The inverse of the unemployment rate is used to approximate the convex relationship between the unemployment rate and the rate of change in wages.* Since labor-market tightness increases as unemployment falls, d is expected to be positive.

GP_t is a dummy variable designed to test whether the wage-price guideposts of the mid-1960s had an impact on wages. The coefficient

---

*The four-quarter percentage change in the unemployment rate, the manufacturing layoff rate, and the unemployment rate for manufacturing were also tried separately and in combination, but all were inferior proxies of labor market tightness.

on GP_t should be negative if the guide posts held down inflation, however slightly, and thereby slowed the rate of increase in wages.

$\overline{TWF}_t$ is the weighted average of the four-quarter rate of change in the ratio of gross wages to wages net of personal tax payments. This is the weighted average of the change in the personal tax multiplier. The tax rate is defined as a ratio with the sum of personal tax payments and employee social security contributions in the numerator and personal income in the denominator. The weights for $\overline{TWF}_t$ are 10.0, -4.5, -3.0, and -1.5. The hypothesis is that an increase in personal taxes leads to an initially higher wage increase in the short run, as workers shift the burden of increased taxes to employers in the form of higher wage increases. However, in the long run most of it is shifted back. Thus, both in the short run and on balance, tax increases would fuel rather than dampen wage changes.

The Price Equation. Equation 2 is

$$PQF = h + i\,(\overline{WF}_{t-1} - .03) + j(WF_t - \overline{WF}_{t-1}) + k\overline{TC}_t$$

where the t subscripts, "bars," and "F" suffixes have the same meaning as in the wage equation.

$\overline{PQF}_t$ is the four-quarter rate of change in the weighted average of output prices for sixteen manufacturing price indexes. The output prices for each two-digit SIC code are weighted by 1955 value of shipments. The industries by SIC code are: food processing (20); tobacco (21); textiles (22); apparel (23); lumber (24); furniture (25); paper (26); chemicals (28); rubber (30); stone, clay, and glass (32); ferrous metals (331); nonferrous metals (333); fabricated metals (34) and instruments (38); nonelectrical machinery (35); electrical machinery (36); and motor vehicles (371). The output prices for each (approximate) two-digit SIC were constructed by Guy, Kraft, and Roberts[6] following the procedure established by Eckstein and Wyss[7]. PQF_t explains 87 percent of the variation in the four-quarter rate of change of WPI for manufacturing ($WPIMF_t$) between 1955:1 and 1972:4.

$$WPIMF = 31.25 + .9003\,PQF_t$$
$$(3.27)\quad(21.63)$$

$$\overline{R}^2 = 0.87; \qquad S.E.E. = .00561; \qquad D.W. = 0.48$$

The large intercept occurs since $WPIMF_t$ is a 1967 base while PQF_t is as 1958 base.

Equation 2 is based on the hypothesis that labor costs are the main driving force behind prices.

The value .03 is the trend value of the four-quarter rate of growth of output per man-hour for the manufacturing sector from 1949:1 to 1969:4

inclusive. $(\overline{WF}_{t-1} - .03)$ is the long-run four-quarter rate of change in standard unit labor costs, where $\overline{WF}_{t-1}$ is a lagged weighted average of the long-run rate of change in manufacturing wages and .03 is the long-run rate of change in labor productivity for manufacturing. The coefficient i for standard unit labor costs should be close to one, based on the observation that, in the long run, total unit costs move closely with unit labor costs and the markup of price over costs remains stable. This view is consistent with the target rate of return pricing hypothesis, which postulates that firms primarily adjust their prices when there is a permanent shift in standard costs.

$(WF_t - \overline{WF}_{t-1})$ indicates whether the current quarterly rate of change in wages is greater than, equal to, or less than the long-run rate of change in wages. The coefficient on this variable should be positive but smaller than i if firms adjust their prices to changes in costs to a lesser degree in the short run than in the long run.

TC_t is the current ratio of corporate tax liabilities to corporate profits before taxes. $\overline{TC}_t$ is the weighted average of the corporate tax rate from period t through t - 3. The coefficient k for $\overline{TC}_t$ should be negative and small, reflecting the fact that the corporate profits tax rate exerts a negative but marginal downward influence on manufacturing price determination in the short run. It is quite possible that in the long run the entire corporate profits tax is entirely shifted onto the consumer in the form of higher prices. However, forms of the corporate tax rate variable with weights reflecting this forward shifting were insignificant, which would imply no influence on pricing in the long run. Since we want to measure the short-run influence of the corporate tax on prices, we have retained the short-run tax influence variable $\overline{TC}_t$.

The short-run impact on an increase in the effective corporate tax rate is a reduction of cash flow. The effective tax rate reduces cash flow, which in turn reduces purchasing power and thereby lessens pressure on prices.

ESTIMATED WAGE AND PRICE EQUATIONS

The results for the estimated wage and price equation appear in Table 6.1. Both the wage and price equations were corrected for auto-correlation using nonlinear least squares estimation and the Hildreth-Lu technique. The Hildreth-Lu technique was used to search a grid of values to insure that the nonlinear estimates were a global minimum rather than only a local minimum for the residual sum of squares. The wage equations were corrected for first order autocorrelation, while the price equations were corrected for second order autocorrelation. We assume the following equation structure

$$Y_t = \sum_i b_i X_i + u_t$$

if the autocorrelation were first order, then $u_t = p \, u_{t-1} + v_t$, where v_t is not autocorrelated. The transformed equation would become

$$y_t = p \, y_{t-1} + \sum_i b_i x_{it} - p \sum_i b_i x_{it-1} + v_t.$$

If the autocorrelation were second order then

$$u_t = p_1 u_{t-1} + p_2 u_{t-1} + v_t$$

where v_t is not autocorrelated. The transformed equation would become

$$y_t = p_1 y_{t-1} + p_2 y_{t-2} + \sum_i b_i x_{it} - p_1 \sum_i b_i x_{it-1} - p_2 \sum_i b_i x_{it-2}$$

$$+ \, v_t$$

In either case the regressions were estimated by a nonlinear regression, and then checked by the Hildreth-Lu search. The equations were estimated from the third quarter of 1959 through the second quarter of 1971 so as to exclude the controls program.

By correcting for autocorrelation we have eliminated the problem of underestimating the variances of the regression coefficients. The autocorrelation coefficients were all significantly different from zero at the 5 percent level of confidence, which indicates that failure to correct for serial correlation would produce unduly large variances of the regression coefficients and inefficient predictions. [8]

All coefficients in the wage equation have the correct signs and are significant at the 5 percent level of confidence except PCF_t and $\overline{TWF_t}$. The insignificance of the coefficient on PCF_t appears to stem from its multicollinearity with $PCFEXP_{t-1}$. The significance of $PCFEXP_{t-1}$ demonstrates the importance of pure expectations in the determination of wages.

In normal times 36 percent of the annual rise in consumer prices is passed into higher wages and the remaining 64 percent is absorbed by the workers. However, in times of price inflation of more than 5 percent in the preceding two years, the coefficients on PCF_t and $PCFEXP_{t-1}$ imply that 90 percent of an increase in the rate of inflation will be passed on by the workers within one year and 144 percent within two years.

Although the employee tax variable is insignificant, the size of the coefficient indicates that changes in employee taxes have a marginal influence on the determination of wages. It appears that while workers are successful in obtaining initial wage increases, their position is eroded because a portion of the burden is shifted from the employer back onto the employee. The net influence is extremely small, and

TABLE 6.1

Regressions Results for Manufacturing, 1959:3-1971:2
(t statistic in parenthesis)

Wage equation: parameter estimates

a	b	c	d	e	f	p_1
.0129	.360	.547	.094	-.005	.016	.286
(2.00)	(1.16)	(2.17)	(1.93)	(-2.04)	(1.60)	(1.80)

$\overline{R}^2$ = .88; D.W.* = 1.99; S.E.E. = .00552

Price equation: parameter estimates

h	i	j	k	p_2	p_3
.093	1.03	.206	-.208	1.312	.554
(1.91)	(6.17)	(3.06)	(-1.88)	(10.46)	(-4.32)

$\overline{R}^2$ = .94; D.W.* = 2.04; S.E.E. = .00377

Note: Abbreviations are as follows:
$\overline{R}^2$ Corrected coefficient of determination
D.W.*   Durbin Watson statistic after correcting for autocorrelation
S.E.E.   Standard error of the estimate
p_1 Autocorrelation coefficients
p_2, p_3 Autocorrelation coefficients (second order)

workers are only successful in shifting 1.6 percent of any tax increase onto their employers.

The estimated price equation indicates that labor costs and taxes are the most influential variables in explaining prices. The coefficient on standard unit labor costs is greater than, but not statistically different from, one that is consistent with a target-rate-of-return pricing hypothesis. The coefficient on the difference in the rate of growth of current and intermediate labor costs is smaller than that of standard unit labor costs. This implies that firms partially adjust prices to factor costs at some intermediate period, which conforms to the adjustment mechanism previously expected. This could also support the hypothesis that, as an aggregate, firms in the manufacturing sector operate on a target-rate-of-return hypothesis and adjust prices in an intermediate period in order to achieve their target rate.

The coefficient of the effective corporate tax rate is significant and does appear to influence price movements. The magnitude of the coefficient for the tax variable suggests that a one-point change in the effective tax rate (say from 25 to 26 percent) would reduce prices by about .2 percentage points.

Stability tests. Each of the equations were tested for stability of the coefficients over the 1959:3-1965:4 and 1966:1-1971:2 subperiods. The coefficients of the price equations were unstable across subperiods, while the wage equation coefficients were stable.

Simulations. Since wages and prices interact simultaneously, the wage and price equations should not be interpreted separately. Rather, the simultaneous interaction of wages and prices allowing for feedback should be considered. In order to permit the simultaneous determination of wages and prices, we simulated our model over the 1959:3-1971:2 period with the estimated equations presented in Table 6.1. We then measured the accuracy of the simulations to determine the model's performance in the precontrol period.

For the manufacturing wage and price equations to capture the feedback dynamics of the inflation process, it is necessary that the wages and prices be treated as endogenous variables. Wages (WF_t) are endogenous in our model, and output prices (PQF_t) are also endogenous in our model. However, PCF_t is presently exogenous. To close the model, PCF_t will become endogenous by making consumer prices (PCF_t) a function of output prices (PQF_t). The equation linking consumer prices (PCF_t) to output prices (PQF_t) is estimated for the period 1959:3-1971:2 by using an Almon lag structure. Our estimated equation implies that the partial adjustment mechanism is such that eight quarters are required for 96 percent of output prices to be translated into input prices. The linking equation (Equation 3)[*] is

$$PCF_t = \underset{(14.62)}{0.01161} + \underset{(21.21)}{0.95212} \sum_{i-o}^{7} PQF_{t-i}$$

$\overline{R}^2 = .91$;   D.W. $= 0.412$;   S.E.E. $= .00410$.

Table 6.2 reports several error measures for the simulation of manufacturing wages and prices over the period 1959:3-1971:2. The model tracks quite well. For both wages and prices there is a slight average overprediction of .02 percent for wages and .75 percent for prices.

The mean absolute error indicates that at each discrete simulation the average error, irrespective of sign, is .44 percent for wages and .55 percent for prices. When compared with the means of each series, this error is quite small. The Theil U statistic is constrained to an interval from zero to one with values below .3, implying a fairly accurate forecasting ability. Both the simulated wages and prices have values in this range.

[*]We use a second degree polynomial lag with the coefficient constrained to zero in the last period. Equation 3 presents the sum of the lag coefficients on PQF_t, where the t statistic is computed from the standard error for the sum.

TABLE 6. 2

Error Measures for Simulations, 1959:3-1971:2

	WF_t	PQF_t
Mean error	-.000230	-.001547
Mean absolute error	.004429	.005534
Root mean square error	.005248	.006679
Theil U Statistic	.057157	.170945

Note: The Mean of WF_t is .043284, and the mean of PQF_t is .045655.

TABLE 6. 3

Simulation of the Precontrols Model from 1971:3
through 1972:4 for an Economy without Controls

	Simulated Values for an Economy without Controls		Actual Values for an Economy with Controls	
	WF_t	PQF_t	WF_t	PQF_t
1971:3	6.99	3.68	6.56	3.98
1971:4	6.49	4.20	6.89	3.71
1972:1	6.21	3.99	6.15	4.23
1972:2	5.82	3.70	6.17	3.69
1972:3	5.48	3.36	6.11	3.29
1972:4	5.26	3.04	6.88	3.68

The mean error is computed by taking the mean of the difference of actual value and the simulated value; the mean absolute error is the mean of the absolute values of the difference of the actual and simulated value. The root mean square error is an estimate of the standard deviation of the residuals of the simulation. [9] The standard deviation of the residuals of the simulated wage and price equations are quite close to the standard error of estimates reported for the equations in Table 6. 1. [10]

If we assume that our precontrol wage and price model accurately represents the mechanism generating wages and prices, then the simulation of the precontrol model over the period from 1971:3 to 1972:4 should produce estimates of the movement of wages and prices in the absence of wage and price controls. This assumes that the wage and price control system had no effect on exogenous variables such as the unemployment rate, productivity, and the effective tax rates. The difference between the forecasted values and the actual values that occurred during the period of control would be an approximation of the total impact of the controls on the determination of wages and prices in the manufacturing sector. In solving the historical precontrol model from 1971:3 through 1972:4, we are assuming that wages and prices are generated by the same mechanism as they were prior to controls. The difference between wages and prices for an economy with controls (actual values) and without controls (simulated values) implies that wages rose by .42 percent more than they would have risen in the absence of controls and that prices rose .10 percent more than they would have in the absence of controls. Table 6.3 compares actual and simulated values. However, this is a rough approximation for the total impact of controls on manufacturing wages and prices.

CONTROLS AND LONG-RUN ADJUSTMENT

In the previous section we provided an approximation of the total impact of the Economic Stabilization Program by comparing the interaction of simulated wages and prices for an economy without controls with the actual wages and prices for an economy with controls. An alternative is to estimate the direct impact of the controls program by including variables in the wage and price equations that serve as proxies for the 90-day freeze and Phase II. We introduced into the equations a dummy variable, ESP_t, which takes the value of one for all observations during the period of controls and the value of zero for all other observations.

Empirical results. The coefficient on ESP_t in the reestimated wage and price equations provides a measure of the marginal impact of controls on manufacturing wages and prices. It may be interpreted as the partial derivative of changes in wages and prices with respect to the actions of the Economic Stabilization Program. Dummy variables measure the impact on the residuals of an estimated equation. In our circumstance we have associated this impact with the establishment of controls.[11] However, the dummy variable could capture other unspecified influences.

The reestimated equations appear in Table 6.4. In examining the equations the coefficients for ESP_t (respectively g and n) indicate that controls exerted direct upward pressure on both manufacturing wages and output prices.

The equations of Table 6.4 provide a measure of the direct impact of the controls program on wages and prices because the individual equations are incapable of picking up the feedback dynamics until simulated as a simultaneous system of equations.

Stability tests. The equations were tested for stability of the coefficients
over the 1959:3-1965:4 and 1966:1-1972:4 subperiods; and the 1959:3-
1971:2 and 1971:3-1972:4 subperiods. The wage equation coefficients
were stable across both subperiods, while the price equations were
unstable over the 1959:3-1965:4 and 1966:1-1971:2 subperiods but stable
over the 1959:3-1971:2 and 1971:3-1972:4 subperiods. *

Simulations. Simulations of the reestimated model for the period from
1959:3 to 1972:4 provides an indication of how well the model performs.
The error measures can then be compared with the precontrols simulation.
The error measures for the reestimated model appear in Table 6.5. The
Theil U Statistics and root mean square errors all indicate that our
reestimated models track fairly well.
   The estimated regression coefficients of ESP_t are a measure of the
direct impact of controls on the economy and fail to take account of the
interaction of wages and prices. In an earlier section of this chapter we
attempted to determine the total impact of controls by comparing the
predicted values as generated by a simulation for an economy without
controls with the actual values produced by an economy operating under
the constraint of controls. By comparing the simulated values for an
economy without controls against the actual values for an economy
with controls, we are either overstating or understating total impact
due to the presence of bias in the simulated series. To correct this
we should simulate the reestimated model from 1971:3 to 1972:4 with
the ESP_t variable. We then set ESP_t equal to zero and simulate from
1971:3 to 1972:4. The former case is the solution for an economy with
controls and the latter is the solution for an economy without controls.
The difference between these two simulations is a measure of the total
impact of the controls program when we assume that any bias is subtracted out. Our results indicate that controls resulted in manufacturing
wages that were 1.8 percent higher annually than would have occurred in
the absence of controls and prices that were 1.79 percent higher annually
than in the absence of controls.
   There are several explanations for this positive impact. Very few
labor contracts were negotiated in the manufacturing sector during Phase
II. Thus many workers received wage increases that were negotiated
prior to August 15, 1971. The second- and third-year increases for
manufacturing contracts anticipated continuing high rates of inflation.
Second, those contracts negotiated in Phase II were usually qualified

---

*The computation of stability tests for the 1959:3-1971:2 and 1971:3-
1972:4 subperiods have insufficient degrees of freedom. For a correction
of this problem see Franklin M. Fisher, "Tests of Equality between Sets
of Coefficients in Two Linear Regressions: An Expository Note," Econo-
metrica 38, no. 2 (March 1970): 361-66.

TABLE 6.4

Regression Results for Manufacturing,
with Controls, 1959:3-1972:4
(t statistic in parenthesis)

Wage equation: parameter estimates

a	b	c	d	e	f	g	p_1
.0149	.539	.328	.0748	-.00611	.00708	.0132	.126
(2.60)	(1.87)	(1.49)	(1.69)	(-2.77)	(0.64)	(3.87)	(2.81)

$\overline{R}^2$ = .88; D.W.* = 1.92: S.E.E. = .00578

Price equation: parameter estimates

h	i	j	k	n	p_2	p_3
.0821	1.01	.135	-.185	.00377	1.31	-.558
(1.87)	(7.25)	(2.26)	(-1.83)	(1.13)	(11.00)	(-4.64)

$\overline{R}^2$ = .95; D.W.* = 2.01; S.E.E. = .00363

Note: Abbreviations are as follows:
$\overline{R}^2$ — Corrected coefficient of determination
D.W.* — Durbin Watson Statistic after correcting for autocorrelation
S.E.E. — Standard error of estimate
p_1 — Autocorrelation coefficient
p_2, p_3 — Autocorrelation coefficients (second order)

TABLE 6.5

Error Measures for ESP_t Simulation, 1959:3-1972:4

	WF_t	PQF_t
Mean error	-.001547	-.001279
Mean absolute error	.005534	.007474
Root mean square error	.006923	.008875
Theil U statistic	.070495	.193738

Note: The mean of WF_t is .045655 and the mean of PQF_t is .046050.

by catch-up clauses or parity adjustments for previous losses in real income. Third, the Pay Board guidelines may have been higher than union targeted wage demands. On the price side, the push in wages may have forced up prices. It is well known that the controls caused some price distortions and supply shortages that were not expected.

Controls versus Tax Policy. It appears that the controls program had no impact, direct or total, on holding down wages and prices in the manufacturing sector. While others have found that controls influenced wages and prices in the private nonfarm economy, controls appear to have been a failure in the very sector they were designed to influence. [12] If tax policy had been used to fight inflation, the net benefits to society from a stabilization program might have been greater.

From an examination of the partial derivatives of the wage and price equations, it seems that a more direct effect on prices could be obtained by changing the corporate tax rate, a 1 percent change would reduce prices by about .2 percent. This reduction stems from reduced cash flow and the lessening of demand pressure on prices. When coupled with the feedbacks of the wage and price mechanism, wages would have been reduced. Although we found no significant evidence of shifts in the corporate tax rate, evidence probably will appear at some later date. However, the important question is whether changing the corporate tax rate would have some immediate, short-run, lasting impact on the Phillips curve. The purpose of controls was to have a short-run temporary impact on wages and prices and thereby slow inflation as the economy adjusted to an equilibrium position. Our analysis would indicate that controls exerted no downward pressure on inflation in the manufacturing sector. We can compare the short-run impact of controls and tax policy by determining the impact of such policies on the long-run price-unemployment trade-off.

Solving the wage and price equations simultaneously under appropriate steady-state assumptions yields the long-run Phillips curves. Our solution is based on the following assumptions: (1) all prices change in the same proportion; (2) tax rates do not change; (3) product-market excess demand conditions do not change; (4) there are no guideposts; (5) wages, prices, and productivity have been growing long enough for initial conditions and lag structures to have no impact.

The above assumptions are used to determine the long-run equilibrium price-umemployment tradeoff for three conditions: (1) an economy without controls and with a constant effective tax rate; (2) an economy with controls and with a constant effective rax rate; and (3) an economy without controls and with adjustments in the effective corporate tax rate that will cause it to increase by ten points and remain fixed thereafter.

The long-run Phillips curve solution for manufacturing prices with the program (Equation 4) is

$$\dot{PQF}_t = .1809 + .1605 \ (1/u)$$

and without the program (Equation 5)

$$\dot{PQF}_t = .1160 + .1406 \ (1/u).$$

By increasing the tax rate the equilibrium solution (Equation 6) is

$$\dot{PQF}_t = .1109 + .1406 \ (1/u).$$

From the equilibrium solutions we see that a 10 percent change in the effective corporate tax rate will reduce the output price of manufacturing by .51 percent in the long run This would imply that an increase in the corporate tax would reduce prices slightly.

Simulation of the precontrol model with a 10 percent increase in the effective corporate tax rate implies prices were reduced by .48 percent annually and wages were reduced .21 percent annually for the period 1971:3-1972:4. Thus, changing the corporate tax rate would have a slight influence on the determination of prices in manufacturing and an even lesser impact on wages.

SUMMARY

Based on our findings, the corporate tax rate influences the determination of price changes in manufacturing but would be a poor policy tool to control inflation. Our analysis was based on a nonshifting corporate tax rate that could be changed at will. Assuming that the corporate tax can be shifted onto the consumer and that there are time lags in obtaining a corporate tax increase, its impact on reducing inflation may be zero or close to zero, irrespective of the small absolute shift in the Phillips curve. Timing and shifting of personal taxes would preclude them as a policy tool, although the personal tax multiplier had an extremely small and insignificant coefficient in our wage equation.

Although our analysis shows that neither policy tool is very effective, it would appear that the negligible positive benefits of a tax increase may be better than the negative benefits of the controls program. [13] It seems that tax increases become permanent, while controls are supposed to be temporary.

NOTES

1. For similar assumptions concerning the measurement of taxes in wage and price equations see William R. Moffat, "Taxes in the Price Equation: Textiles and Rubber, " Review of Economics and Statistics 50, no. 3 (August 1970), 253-61.

2. Otto Eckstein and Roger Brinner, The Inflation Process in the United States, United States Joint Economic Committee of Congress, 92nd cong., 2nd sess. (Washington, D. C.: Government Printing Office, 1972). Otto Eckstein and Gary Fromm, "The Price Equation, " American Economic Review 48, no. 5 (December 1968): 1159-83; Ben E. Laden, "Perfect Competition, Average Cost Pricing and the Price Equation, " Review of Economics and Statistics 54, no. 1 (February 1972): 84-88.

3. Otto Eckstein and Thomas A. Wilson, "The Determination of Money Wages in American Industry, " Quarterly Journal of Economics 86 (August 1962): 379-414; Edwin Kuh, "A Productivity Theory of Wage Levels—An Alternative to the Phillips Curve, " Review of Economic Studies 34, no. 100 (October 1967): 333-60; George L. Perry, "The Determinants of Wage Rate Changes and the Inflation-Unemployment Trade-Off for the United States, " Review of Economic Studies 31, no. 88 (October 1964), 287-308.

4. L. A. Dicks-Mireaux, "The Interrelationship between Cost and Price Changes, 1946-1959, " Oxford Economic Papers, new series 13, no. 3 (October 1961), 267-92; Eckstein and Brinner, op cit.; Robert J. Gordon, "Inflation in Recession and Recovery, " Brookings Papers on Economic Activity, no. 1 (1971), pp. 105-66.

5. For a different specification of private nonfarm equations, see A. Bradley Askin, and John Kraft, Econometric Wage and Price Models (Lexington, Mass.: D. C. Heath and Lexington Books, 1973) pp. 4-5; Robert J. Gordon, "Wage-Price Controls and the Shifting Phillips Curve, " Brookings Papers on Economic Activity, no. 2 (1972), pp. 385-430, p. 390.

6. Charles Guy, John Kraft, and Blaine Roberts, "The Price Control Experiment: Short Run Success and Long Run Failure? An Econometric Examination of Wages, Prices, and Profit Margins in Sixteen Manufacturing Industries, " (mimeo).

7. Otto Eckstein and David Wyss, "Industry Price Equations, " The Econometrics of Price Determination/Conference (Washington, D. C.: Board of Governors, Federal Reserve System, 1972).

8. On the subject of inefficient predictions, see Jan Kmenta, Elements of Econometrics (New York: MacMillan, 1971). p. 156.

9. Kmenta, op. cit.

10. Henri Theil, Economic Forecasts and Policy (Amsterdam: North Holland Publishing Company, 1965).

11. For a similar interpretation see Barry Bosworth, "Phase II: The U. S. Experiment with an Incomes Policy, " Brookings Papers on Economic Activity, no. 2 (1972), pp. 343-83; Askin and Kraft, op. cit.

12. For an examination of the private nonfarm economy see Bosworth, op. cit.; Gordon, "Inflation in Recession and Recovery, " op. cit.; Askin and Kraft, op. cit.

13. For a benefit cost analysis of the control program see Robert Lanzillotti and Blaine Roberts, "An Assessment of the U. S. Experiment with an Incomes Policy, " paper presented at the Tulane University Conference on Incomes Policies, April 1973.

CHAPTER

7

AN INDUSTRIAL EXAMINATION OF WAGE AND PRICE CONTROLS

Charles Guy, John Kraft,
Blaine Roberts

In this chapter we take an intensive look at the impact of wage and price controls on 16 manufacturing industries during Phase II of the Economic Stabilization Program. The analysis is limited to the impact of controls during Phase II, since this was the only period of extensive and unambiguous wage and price controls. Phase III was in essence a period of voluntary restraint for most industries, and while in some aspects more restrictive wage and price controls were reinstated in Phase IV, the hallmark of this period was sector-by-sector decontrol of the economy and a graceful exit from wage and price controls.

Phase II price controls were based upon two fundamental strategies, the first of which was based on allowable costs and the second based on a profit-margin constraint. Unfortunately, at the time Phase II began (November 1971), there were few empirical or theoretical studies that gave the Price Commission a basis upon which to judge the potential effectiveness of the price control regulations in attaining the goal of a 2.5 percent rate of inflation by the end of 1972. The most notable empirical studies of industry price equations were Eckstein and Wyss,[1] upon whose work this study is built, and Heien and Popkin.[2]

DATA AND ESTIMATION PROCEDURE

Except for the indexes of output and input prices, the data used in this study are published series at the two-digit Standard Industrial Classification (SIC) level of compilation.[3]

In the first case, that of the index of output prices, the correspondence among the monthly elements of the non-seasonally-adjusted wholesale price index (WPI) and three- and four-digit SICs is established at the four-digit level. Weighting by shipments of the corresponding SIC category in 1958, these WPIs were then aggregated to input-output classifications of the 1958 Input-Output Table published in the <u>Survey of Current Business</u>, 44, no. 9 (U.S. Department of Commerce, Washington, 1964). The quarterly series was constructed as a simple average of the monthly series.

The index of input prices was based mainly on output price indexes by using input-output coefficients as weights. The input price for an industry is simply the weighted average of the output prices, where the weights are the direct input requirements as given in the 1958 Input-Output Table. An allowance was also made for intraindustry purchase of important materials from outside manufacturing.

The computation and meaning of the other variables used is straightforward. None of the data used were seasonally adjusted except the profit-and-sales series for ferrous metals, which had to be adjusted to correct for a change in classification.

Four-quarter percentage rates of change (current, lagged, or weighted lagged values) were used in estimating the price- and profit-margin equations. Rates of change are preferable to the level of the variables because of a high degree of multicollinearity among the variables, caused by the fact that the variables are actually simultaneously determined. For example, it is incorrect to think of wage rates as determining price levels. There is actually a feedback process among these variables (and others) in response to common forces at work within the economic system, such as changes in the level of aggregate demand or changes in the rate of unemployment.

All estimated equations were corrected for first- and second-order autocorrelation if present, by a combination of the Hildreth-Lu estimation technique and a nonlinear estimation. The Hildreth-Lu technique was used to search over a grid of values to ensure that the nonlinear estimates were a global minimum rather than only a local minimum for the residual sum of squares.

EQUATION SPECIFICATION

<u>Price Equation.</u> Price adjustment, particularly in the short run, is conceptually a function of many variables. In dealing with rather broad market aggregates, the most notable factor is unit cost changes, that is, factor price increases less factor productivity gains. Also important are market characteristics at a given point in time, such as (1) the degree of excess demand and its perceived permanence; (2) the elasticity of demand as seen by the individual firms; (3) the current productive capacity and the marginal costs associated with greater or lesser output; (4) the costs of price changes, such as the cost of changing a price list or an advertising plan; (5) the reliability and speed of information

flows; (6) the motivations of buyers and sellers, including whether they are profit maximizing, sales maximizing, or nonprofit institutions, or buying for final consumption or as inputs into other productive processes; (7) the ease of entry and exit; and (8) other "institutional" factors such as support prices, international markets and foreign policy, national defense subsidies, and regulation by various governmental bodies.

All of the above factors depend, in turn, upon other aspects of the exchange process. The degree of excess demand depends upon changing preferences, income, other price changes, and/or the state of technology. The elasticity of demand as seen by a firm depends upon a complex interaction of market demand and market structure (from pure competition to monopoly), coupled with an institutional ethic that has developed concerning various forms of price discrimination (from multiple prices to perfect price discrimination) and other marketing practices. Technology and past investment in an industry will partially determine current capacity and the marginal costs of altered production.

The cost of a price change will differ among commodities as the length of the production process, the stage of production, the perishability of the products and the consequent costs of inventory accumulation, and the rate of both physical and technological obsolesence differ. [4] This includes both explicit price changes and implicit price changes through quality variation.

The flow of information in the market will depend upon the number of buyers and sellers; the integrity of "the" market; and a number of institutional factors such as organization, entrepreneurship, and the existence of related markets, such as futures markets. Technology, capital intensity, degree of risk, and legal sanctions will influence the ease of entry and exit. In this mixed society, altered production is, at times, not an alternative in the short run.

Given all of these factors plus a number of others that could be touched upon, one thing that is clear is that one would expect, among manufacturing industries aggregated at the two-digit level, a good deal of difference in those consistent relations that would be identified by a regression equation. Furthermore, most of the above factors lack available quantitative measures. Since these aspects are continuously interacting, there exists no neat hypothesis that can be tested with the available data. For example, rate-of-return pricing by a monopolist could generate the same empirical information as a purely competitive industry, providing there was a similarity among the other factors influencing the price adjustment process. The significance of a rate-of-return variable in the regression equation explaining quarterly changes in prices is probably more a function of the financial characteristics of the production process than the degree of competition or the actual motivations (including profit maximization, sales maximization, and entry barring pricing) that generate price adjustment.

This line of reasoning is not meant to denigrate the value of theory in formulating and organizing knowledge, providing insight for additional testing and control measures, or generally aiding the scientific method; what it does argue is that in the case of price adjustment the theory and the available data are so far apart that meaningful tests cannot be performed—but the identification of stable relations does have value. To the extent that the period of estimation is indicative of future stable institutional factors, the equations add significantly to knowledge of timing of price increases.

The basic form of the price equation estimated (Equation 1) is

$$dp/p = a_0 + a_1 dy/y + a_2 dx/x + a_3 dw/w + a_4 dv/v + a_5 dr/r + a_6 di/i$$

where p is an index of the price of output; y is an output variable; x is an excess demand variable; w is a wage rate variable; v is an index of materials prices; r is a rate-or-return variable; and i is an interest variable.

If a_1 is positive, this would indicate that firms take advantage of increased realized demand to raise prices. If the profit margin equation also shows that price increases raise margins, then either economies of scale are present or price increases are in excess of average cost increases due to increased capacity utilization. A negative value of a_1 would imply that economies of scale were being passed on in the form of lower prices, particularly if the profit margin equation shows a zero or positive relation between output and margins.

The coefficient for excess demand variables (such as the ratio of unfilled orders to sales), a_2, would probably be positive if significant. A positive sign would suggest that firms reduce excess demand by raising prices. However, it is not too difficult to imagine a negative relation between excess demand and price adjustment with a high elastic demand and large economies of scale.

A positive value for a_3, the wage coefficient, represents the pass-through of labor cost increases. If a_3 is not significantly different from zero, then either wage increases are not creating average cost increases—that is, productivity advances equal wage advances—or the firm is absorbing such cost increases and recouping them when other costs, such as inputs, change.

A positive sign on a_4 imples that materials cost increases are passed through. A negative value would not be expected, since this would mean that output prices decline as materials costs increase.

There should be a positive relation between price and the rate of return: higher prices should inevitably cause higher rates of return. However, using the rate-of-return variable as an independent variable to explain price adjustments proposes that a change in the rate of return causes prices to be changes. If this is the case, then one would expect a negative sign for a_5; that is, a fall in the rate of return causes prices to be increased, indicating a motivation to maintain a given rate of return. Of course, it is again possible for demand and cost conditions to be such that a fall (rise) in the rate of return would cause prices to fall (rise), especially if demand were elastic and average costs constant, but this is considered unlikely.

The rate of interest coefficient a6, if significant, probably is related to particular financial characteristics in the industry. For firms that have costs (implicit or explicit) that are highly dependent upon rates of interest, one would expect a positive relation: increased costs are passed along as higher prices.

Wage Equation. The theoretical and empirical literature on the determination of wages is richly endowed. The recent flurry of intellectual activity stems from A. W. Phillips, and some of the major contributors have included Richard Lipsey, Otto Eckstein and Thomas A. Wilson, Charles Schultze and Joseph Tryon, Edwin Kuh, Milton Friedman, George Akerlof, and Edmund S. Phelps. [5] The major issues can be broadly summarized as follows: Is there a tradeoff between the level of unemployment and the rate of change in wages; and if so, is this tradeoff of a short-run or a long-run nature?

The evidence for a short-run tradeoff between wage change and the level of unemployment is fairly clear, but the debate over the long-run tradeoff can be divided into two camps, one holding that a long-run convex tradeoff exists[6] and the second that the long-run Phillips curve is vertical and coincident with the natural rate of unemployment. [7]

One of the primary reasons given for the existence of a short-run tradeoff is the lack of perfect information in the labor market. This line of reasoning argues that tighter labor markets and rapidly increasing wages improve the flows of information and thus enable the labor market to work more efficiently; for instance, the unemployment rate is lowered. Friedman and Phelps, in particular, have argued that the improved information is only generated because things are not the same as expected; hence the maintenance of a lower than natural level of unemployment requires successively higher rates of inflation, higher than expected. Since this outcome is untenable in the long run, the system must eventually return to the natural rate of unemployment, if not a higher level. On the other hand, Akerlof presents a simple model where a desired relative wage structure is bargained at different times. This "institutional rigidity" does generate a long-run, convex relation between unemployment and the rate of change in wages, even when expectations are fully realized.

Arthur Okun[8] has also presented a theoretical structure that generates a Phillips curve world.

Other factors that contribute to wage inflation have been variously identified as monopoly power, both on the part of particular firms and particular unions; productivity differentials leading to higher than

average wage increases in particular industries that are then emulated
by all other sectors; "spillover," thesis which is similar to the productivity differential; and the consequences of the battle over relative
shares between capital and labor.

We are principally interested in the development of wage equations
for sixteen manufacturing industries. While the literature is voluminous,
it is not rich in wage equations, by industry, that can be used to assess
the impact (actual or potential) of wage-price controls. [9]

Ideally the exogenous variables are industry demand, and hence
industry employment; changes in employment in other industries; changes
in wages in other industries; and relative rates of productivity. The
primary objective here is the estimation of wage equations that accurately predict wage changes based upon past empirical evidence. Thus,
several modifications are necessary in the transition from the theoretical to the empirical. First, employment for each two-digit industry
is available, but to capture employment in all other industries it is
probably desirable to use the aggregate rate of unemployment, since
the labor force and labor force participation rate are not constant over
time. This can be further supplemented by the level of layoffs and
output per man-hour for all manufacturing, since these data are not
available by industry. Output per man-hour for all manufacturing could
be used for industries that are large or that for some other reason have
productivity rates highly correlated with the productivity rate for manufacturing as a whole. Under the assumption that prices reflect changes
in unit labor costs, an appropriate variable for changes in wages would
be an aggregate price index. The Consumer Price Index and the level
of industry profits were chosen as proxies. This institutional ethic can
be further approximated by adding a variable that permits a catch-up
when such aggregates are misjudged by the bargaining parties. Another
consideration is necessary as well: when significant labor saving
changes are introduced, the result is a higher-quality worker with a
commensurately higher wage rate. Therefore, in industries where such
investments have taken place over time, one would expect a deviation
from the rate of aggregate productivity and consequently a negative
relation between the rate of change in industry employment and changes
in average hourly earnings.

The general form of the equation estimated for each industry
(Equation 2) is as follows:

$$dw/w = a_o + a_1 \, dp/p + a_2 \, dE/E + a_3 \, dQ/Q + a_4 \, 1/U + a_5 \, Z$$

$$+ a_6 L + a_7 GPD$$

where w is the industry wage rate; p is the Consumer Price Index; E is
the industry employment; Q is the productivity index for all manufac-

turing; U is the aggregate rate of unemployment; Z is the level of industry profits; L is the layoff rate for all manufacturing; and GPD is a guidepost dummy variable (its values are 1962:1, .25; 1962:2, .5; 1962:3, .75;1962:4 to 1966:4, 1; 1967:1, .75; 1967:2, .5; 1967:3, .25; zero all other quarters).

Profit Margin Equations. Profit margins are, by definition, a function of output price, level of output, and unit (or average) costs of production. Essentially they are a residual of what happens to other variables. As such, equations that explain changes in profit margins do not suffer from the same theoretical morass of confluent unmeasurables as optimal price adjustment. They do, however, suffer from inadequate profit data. The values of the parameters in the profit margin equation do tell us something about the industry. Furthermore, in cases of sufficiently small standard error such equations should also be useful to assess the potential impact of a system of price controls that relies, in part, upon a profit margin limitation. The estimated profit margin equation (Equation 3) is

$$\frac{dm}{m} = a_Q + a_1 dy/y + a_2 dp/p + a_3 dw/w + a_4 dv/v + a_5 dr/r + a_6 dk/k$$

where m is the ratio of pretax profits to sales; y is output; p is the output price; w is the wage rate; v is the materials price; r is the rate of interest; and k is depreciation.

The output coefficient a_1 would be expected not to be negative. If a_1 were positive, economies of scale would be indicated, and firms in that industry would stabilize prices, in that margins would expand as output increases and contract as output contracts. If a_1 were zero, either average costs would be constant or firms would lower prices as output expanded and raised prices as output contracted in the case of economies of scale. The reverse would follow for diseconomies of scale. Whichever the case, the firms would be following a more competitive model if a_1 were approximately zero. If a_2, the output price coefficient, is not significant, then price changes can be inferred to be responsive to average cost changes: price changes do not cause margins to rise or fall. A positive coefficient would imply that firms were exploiting increased demand; that is, raising prices in response to unit cost changes but not sufficiently to make up for average cost increases. If a_2 were negative, one would expect to find a_1 positive; that is, the loss in margins accompanying cost increases with output constant is made up for by increasing production. This combination ($a_2 < 0$, $a_1 > 0$) would be a greater stabilization of prices than $a_1 > 0$ and $a_2 = 0$.

The sign of the wage coefficient a_3 would indicate whether wage increases exceed gains in output per manhour ($a_3 < 0$) or whether productivity gains were greater than wage increases ($a_3 > 0$) when output is held constant. A combination of $a_2 > 0$ and $a_3 > 0$ would be a lagged response of price increases to wage increases that exceed productivity gains. On the other hand, $a_2 < 0$ and $a_3 > 0$ would suggest that price increases do not make up for average-unit-cost increases and that wage increases are used as an excuse to raise prices above the level of the increased wage bill. In this case one would expect a_4, the materials price coefficient, to be insignificant.

If a_4 were positive, materials price increases would be in excess of their actual impact on unit costs. This could occur if firms exploited an outward shift in demand and also passed it back through higher prices for materials. A negative sign for a_4 would indicate that the manufacturer stabilizes prices; a negative sign can be expected in a case in which materials prices fluctuate widely about a rather constant mean, such as in food processing or perhaps in textiles.

If a_5, the interest rate coefficient, were negative, the firms would be stabilizing prices by not passing along increased interest costs or reducing prices when interest rates fell. It is also possible that net interest would be positive for the firms, in which case increased interest rates would raise profits without affecting sales proportionately. The coefficient a_5 would be positive if firms passed along changes in interest rates on their average costs.

THE IMPACT OF PHASES I AND II ON
PRICES, WAGES, AND PROFIT MARGINS

In this section we will examine the impact of the Economic Stabilization Program by estimating the structural shift that occured in wage, price, and profit margin equations for 16 manufacturing industries. The technique is a simple one. All equations are first estimated from the period 1959:3-1961:2, depending on the lags involved, to 1971:2. This is because some of the data are only available from 1958 and because 1971:2 is the last quarter before Phase I occurred. Next all equations are reestimated, extending the period of estimation from 1971:2 to 1972:4 for our previously estimated equations and adding a dummy variable, the value of which is 0 for 1959:3-1971:2 and 1 for 1971:3-1972:4, to each equation.

Using the estimated coefficient for a dummy variable in a price, wage, or profit margin equation leaves a great deal unanswered about the effect of the program. First, it is only the marginal impact of the program in terms of a structural change that occurred among the independent and dependent variables; that is assuming the program was totally responsible for any change that occurred. Second, to determine the actual impact a model should be constructed that would compare simulated values without controls to simulated values with controls or with actual data. This exercise would be far too complicated and would

TABLE 7.1

Industry Price Equations, 1959:3-1972:4
(t-statistics in parenthesis)

Independent variables		Constant	Output JFRBF UCAPFRBF*	Demand INV%SCF INV%SCF*	Wages AHE[F AHE[F (-1)* AHE[FWA† AHE[FWA (-1)‡ AHE[FWA (-2)+
Industry					
Food processing	20	.0142 (1.85)	—	-.1257 (-2.13)	—
Tobacco	21	.0050 (.51)	—	—	.27270+ (2.08)
Textiles	22	-.0492 (-3.07)	.0764 (1.60)	—	1.277† (3.84)
Apparel	23	.0109 (2.68)	—	—	—
Lumber	24	-.0537 (-1.48)	.5243 (3.20)	—	1.466‡ (2.08)
Furniture	25	-.0079 (-2.68)	—	—	.7406† (10.62)
Paper	26	-.0103 (-1.31)	—	—	.3674 (2.29)
Chemicals	28	-.0083 (-1.08)	—	.0505* (3.70)	.2105* (1.62)
Rubber	30	-.0103 (-.75)	—	—	.7428† (2.18)
Stone, clay, and glass	32	-.0257 (4.49)	—	—	1.070† (8.33)
Ferrous metals	331	—	—	—	—
Nonferrous metals	333	.0125 (.66)	—	-.0596 (1.41)	.38870+ (.91)
Fabricated metals and instruments	348	-.0025 (-1.20)	— —	.0203 (1.81)	.3951† (5.98)
Nonelectrical machinery	35	.0019 (.21)	—	—	.3143† (1.68)
Electrical machinery	36	.0042 (.80)	-.0667* (-2.26)	—	—
Motor vehicles	371	-.0052	—	—	—

Note: Asterisks in the independent variables portion of the table refer to specific coefficients estimated in the equation in the industry-by-industry section below them in each column. Variables are defined in the appendix to this chapter.

Source: Compiled by the author.

Materials PINF PINF (-1)* PINF (-2)† PINF (-4)‡ PINFWA+	Rate of Return of Interest ZADP%EQF (-2) RMAAF*	ESP Dummy	RHOI	RHO2	$\bar{R}^2$	D.W.	S.E.
.3923 (7.41)	—	-.0059 (-.57)	.80	—	.89	1.72	.0106
—	.0967 - .0204* (2.71) (-2.00)	-0204 (-2.00)	.94	-.18	.80	2.02	.0099
.1501 (1.80)	—	.0059 (.62)	1.50	-.80	.91	1.89	.0112
.0570* (1.85)	—	.0079 (2.85)	1.40	-.50	.93	2.05	.0030
—	—	.0758 (2.24)	1.20	-.50	.83	2.23	.0084
.0189† (1.62)	—	-.0036 (-1.17)	1.10	-.50	.94	2.25	.0036
.0531* (2.20)	—	.0091 (1.38)	1.10	-.45	.81	2.00	.0075
—	—	.0011 (.31)	.90	—	.85	1.97	.0036
1.204‡ (3.80)	—	-.0148 (-1.04)	.90	-.20	.77	1.87	.0153
—	—	.0065 (1.17)	1.00	-.38	.94	2.16	.0059
.2277 (1.59)	—	.0319 (4.42)	1.46	-.54	.93	1.81	.0078
—	—	-.0001 (.00)	1.40	-.70	.85	1.79	.0230
.4430 (8.66)	—	-.0001 (-.04)	.80	-.40	.97	1.89	.0028
.3610 (3.03)	—	.0001 (.03)	.90	—	.95	1.93	.0034
—	—	.0006 (.09)	1.40	-.60	.89	1,85	.0076
.8363+ (4.65)	—	.0037 (.45)	.85	-.25	.80	2.16	.0094

TABLE 7. 2
Industry Profit Margin Equations, 1959:3-1972:4
(t-statistics in parenthesis)

Independent Variables		Constant	Output JFRBF	Demand CNCS58F	Price PQF PQF(-1)*	Wages AHE[F AHE[F(-1)* AHE[F(-4)† AHE[FWA‡
Industry						
Food processing	20	.0059 (.43)	—	—	-.3524*	—
Tobacco	21	-.0338 (1.80)	.3679 (2.44)	—	1.453* (3.02)	—
Textiles	22	-.0618 (-2.12)	2.687 (7.52)	—	1.599 (2.25)	—
Apparel	23	-.2042 (-2.67)	3.260 (3.32)	1.300 (1.19)	-10.00* (-2.79)	5.863* (3.67)
Lumber	24	-.2457 (-1.70)	6.184 (4.97)	—	1.203 (1.44)	6.573 (2.00)
Furniture	25	-.0748 (-2.08)	3.796 (6.58)	—	—	—
Paper	26	-.0519 (-.63)	2.346 (5.08)	—	1.844 (1.56)	-2.634* (-1.60)
Chemicals	28	-.1777 (-3.91)	1.281 (5.59)	—	-2.554 (-2.21)	1.134 (1.36)
Rubber	30	-.2767 (-4.34)	1.823 (5.63)	—	—	2.671* (1.91)
Stone, clay, and glass	32	-.1033 (-3.21)	2.296 (4.82)	—	—	—
Ferrous metals	331	-.0152 (-.24)	1.728 (7.02)	—	—	-2.401† (-1.60)
Nonferrous metals	333	-.1384 (-1.75)	2.146 (6.33)	—	1.501 (2.47)	-.4316‡ (-.20)
Fabricated metals and instruments	348	-.0790 (-2.32)	2.173 (7.14)	—	—	—
Nonelectrical machinery	35	-.0478 (-1.74)	.9239 (3.69)	—	—	—
Electrical machinery	36	-.0679 (-1.38)	1.474 (4.67)	—	—	—
Motor vehicles	371	-.0586 (-.98)	1.567 (6.45)	—	—	—

Note: Asterisks in the independent variables portion of the table refer to specific estimated coefficients in the industry-by-industry section below them in each column. Variables are defined in the appendix to this chapter.

Source: Compiled by author.

Input Price and Other Costs PINF PINF(-1)* RMAAPF† DPF‡	ESP Dummy	RHOI	RHO2	$\bar{R}^2$	D.W.	S.E.
−	-.0224 (-.76)	.60	−	.42	1.86	.0367
−	-.031 6 (.91)	.60	−	.41	1.97	.0434
-.5754† (-1.71)	-.1420† (-1.71)	.23	−	.75	1.77	.1100
−	-.0282 (-.25)	−	−	.34	1.71	.2106
−	-.1290 (-.59)	.45	−	.68	1.74	.2735
-.5895* (1.41)	.0441 (.39)	−	−	.47	1.59	.2214
−	.1225 (1.94)	.95	-.30	.85	2.07	.0651
−	.0383 (1.24)	.60	−	.74	1.85	.0368
-6.266 (-3.46)	.2213 (2.30)	.25	−	.58	2.01	.1396
−	.0647 (.77)	.30	−	.45	1.96	.1443
−	.3906 (3.04)	.39	−	.57	2.02	.2651
−	.0413 (.27)	.30	−	.58	1.76	.1931
−	.0313 (.51)	.65	−	.76	1.90	.0706
−	.0001 (.00)	.85	-.30	.71	2.00	.0748
-.3497‡ (-1.76)	.0744 (1.00)	.70	−	.64	2.01	.0831
-.7404† (-1.30)	-.1922 (-1.34)	.30	−	.54	2.17	.2367

TABLE 7.3

Industry Wage Equations, 1959:3-1972:4
(t-statistics in parenthesis)

Independent variables		Constant	Prices CPIF CPIF(-1)* CPIFWA† CPIFWA(-1)‡ CPIEXP+	Employment EPF EPFWA*	Productivity JQ%MHMF JQ%MHMF(-1)*	Unemployment 1/U 1/U(-1)*
Industry						
Food processing	20	.0290 (7.93)	.6866* (7.68)	-.1955 (-2.95)	—	—
Tobacco	21	.0146 (1.21)	1.010* (3.18)	-.2374 (-2.80)	.2846* (1.76)	—
Textiles	22	.0048 (.38)	.6112* (4.30)	.2323* (2.46)	—	.0985 (1.46)
Apparel	23	.0682 (4.23)	.7640† (3.43)	—	—	—
Lumber	24	.0294 (3.08)	.9891* (4.24)	.1759 (2.45)	—	—
Furniture	25	-.0159 (-1.78)	.5921* (4.53)	-.0897 (-2.47)	—	.1918 (4.03)
Paper	26	.0305 (14.40)	.6782* (12.98)	-.0500 (-1.43)	—	—
Chemicals	28	.0454 (6.07)	.1955* (1.39)	—	—	—
Rubber	30	.0276 (3.45)	.5547* (2.79)	.1143 (2.05)	—	—
Stone, clay, and glass	32	.0215 (5.57)	.7157*/.2120+ (4.15)/(1.52)	.0274 (2.61)	—	—
Ferrous metals	331	-.0225 (-1.05)	.4667† (1.39)	-.0902* (-2.23)	.7052 (5.01)	.1304 (1.24)
Nonferrous metals	333	.0656 (2.79)	.3215† (1.03)	.1225 (2.24)	.2065 (1.83)	—
Fabricated metals and instruments	348	.0200 (6.29)	.8617* (10.39)	.0257 (1.25)	—	—
Nonelectrical machinery	35	.0218 (7.73)	.8464‡ (11.16)	.0279 (1.69)	—	—
Electrical machinery	36	.0189 (2.46)	.3490‡ (1.82)	-.1118 (-4.02)	—	—
Motor vehicles	371	.0305 (1.30)	.8745‡ (2.85)	.1824 (5.24)	.3281 (1.69)	-.1504 (-1.27)

Note: Asterisks in the independent variables portion of the table refer to specific figures in the industry-by-industry section below them in each column. Variables are defined in the appendix to this chapter.

Source: Compiled by author.

Profits	Layoffs	GPD Dummy	ESP Dummy					
ZA	L	GPD	ESP	RHOI	RHO2	$\bar{R}^2$	D. W.	S. E.
–	–	-.0117 (-3.51)	.0070 (2.07)	.70	–	.94	1.93	.0042
–	–	–	.0067 (.45)	.50	–	.62	1.88	.0194
–	–	–	.0028 (.43)	.40	–	.78	1.87	.0082
–	-.0214 (-3.32)	-.0205 (-2.701)	-.0210 (-2.46)	.50	–	.82	1.67	.0108
–	–	-.0207 (-2.30)	-.0236 (-2.33)	.60	–	.81	1.70	.0110
–	–	–	.0099 (1.77)	.60	–	.91	1.67	.0054
–	–	-.0093 (-4.79)	.0096 (4.08)	.30	–	.94	1.59	.0039
–	–	-.0095 (-1.79)	-.0006 (-.15)	.90	–	.94	1.91	.0039
–	–	0.0234 (-2.99)	0.0221 (-.27)	.60	–	.76	2.23	.0074
–	–	-.0062 (-1.94)	.0100 (2.40)	.40	–	.92	1.84	.0054
–	–	-.0197 (-1.80)	.0466 (3.80)	.50	–	.82	1.51	.0157
–	-.0183 (-1.95)	-.0302 (2.84)	.0298 (2.82)	.60	–	.84	1.77	.0125
–	–	-.0085 (-2.77)	-.0039 (-1.03)	.60	–	.95	1.40	.0036
–	–	-.0091 (-3.26)	.0026 (.84)	.40	–	.93	1.90	.0045
.0100 (2.49)	–	-.0108 (-1.99)	-.0084 (-1.68)	.70	–	.92	1.67	.0054
.0090 (1.81)	–	-.0251 (-2.47)	-.0078 (-.58)	.40	–	.75	2.14	.0164

require too many questionable assumptions to be undertaken here, although aggregate models for the private nonfarm economy have been constructed elsewhere. Those results, along with the results found here, may be used to generate some idea of where any aggregate reduction in the rate of inflation occurred on an industry-by-industry basis.

The impact of wage and price controls on the structure of the industry equations is assessed by estimating each of the 16 industry equations from 1959:3 (or 1961:2) to 1972:4 with a dummy variable taking the value of 1 for 1971:3-1972:4. The results are shown in Tables 7.1, 7.2, and 7.3. In general there is very little change in the value of the coefficients for the independent variables or the general statistical properties of the equations as compared with estimates for the precontrol period.* All equations were tested for a significant guidepost dummy (GPD) and a control dummy (ESP). The guidepost dummy is significant only for some of the wage equations and only retained where significant. The estimates of ESP are shown in Tables 7.1, 7.2, and 7.3 regardless of significance. As noted previously, the coefficient on ESP is an estimate of only the marginal impact of the Economic Stabilization Program. One is cautioned to interpret these coefficients with great care, since other forces may in fact be responsible for the structural change. Also, forces operating in the opposite direction to that of the Stabilization Program may have neutralized any empirically measurable impact of wage and price controls.

Table 7.4 summarizes the cases in which the dummy is significant at the 10 percent level. In general there appears to be very little impact, at least in the negative direction of the control program. In only one industry is the dummy variable significantly negative for price changes and for only three industries with respect to wages. It is negative for the profit margin equation in textiles and motor vehicles. On the other hand, the dummy variable is significantly positive for four industries in the price equation, six industries in the wage equation, and four industries in the profit margin equation.

For the wage equations the dummy variables, if significant, are generally capturing structural shifts from other causes. This is because most of the major contracts in manufacturing were not negotiated during Phases I and II. Most of the contractual increases were deferred increases signed prior to mid-1971. The only areas in which the Pay Board had a major role during the control program were lumber and glass; in both of these industries negotiated settlements were cut back by the Pay Board. However, the cutback is only picked up for lumber;

---

*The results for the precontrol period and the reestimation of the equations for the controls period produced estimates of the coefficients that were rather robust. While the results for the precontrol period are excluded from this paper, they may be obtained from the authors. The variable definitions appear in the appendix to this chapter.

in SIC 32, which contains a good deal more than glass, the dummy variable is significantly positive.

The positive coefficient for ferrous metals is more indicative of the distortion thesis than of the effects of the control program. This wage settlement was negotiated prior to the freeze of August 14, 1971. It is interesting that average hourly earning were "out of line" during the control period by 4. 7 percent, but given this, price increases in ferrous metals were also "out of line" by 3. 2 percent. Furthermore, the profit margin equation suggests that price increases more than compensated for the high wage increase, since the profit margin dummy variable is positive and significant for SIC 331. Paper shows a similar situation: wages exhibited an upward shift during the control period, but prices more than offset this increased cost with a consequent estimated 12 percent upward shift in the profit margin equation. Apparel and lumber are somewhat puzzling. According to the equations, wages were held down in apparel and lumber while prices were pushed above their normal relation with the independent variables, yet there is no impact upon margins. However, this can be explained by the observation that both lumber and apparel use wage increases as a trigger to raise prices, and such wage increases are correlated positively with margins. Thus if wages were held down this would reduce margins. Furthermore, rising prices in apparel that are not due to wage change or picked up by the demand variable have a negative impact on margins. Finally, it is not completely unreasonable that demand was stimulated abnormally during the period. If these industries are increasing-cost industries, then prices may be higher, average cost curves lower, and margins the same as they would have been without controls.

SUMMARY

Briefly stated, the price regulations in operation during Phase II permitted prices to be increased only to the extent that unit costs increased. This was defined to be a weighted average of factor price increases with a trend value for change in output per man-hour being subtracted from wage increases and an estimated volume increase[*]

---

[*]The estimate was the firms' own. If volume was projected to increase 10 percent and fixed costs were 15 percent of total costs, this would constitute a 1. 5 percent reduction in cost increases as allowable for a price increase. Reliance upon each firm for its own estimate of volume increases substantially biased this offset downward. For a discussion of Phase II regulating see Economic Stabilization, Title 6, Code of Federal Regulations (Washington, D. C.: Government Printing Office, 1972).

TABLE 7.4

Equations in which ESP Dummy was Significant
(industries by SIC numbers)

Price Equations		Wage Equations		Prifit Margin Equation	
Positive	Negative	Positive	Negative	Positive	Negative
23	21	20	23	26	22
24		25	24	28	371
26		26	36	30	
331		32		331	
		331			
		333			

multiplied times fixed costs subtracted from the total. This trend is
the average for the 1958-69 period for each four-digit SIC as calculated
by the Price Commission. Wage increases above the standard of the
Pay Board (5.5 percent plus .7 percent for fringe benefits) were not
allowable. Discretionary cost increases, especially for overhead
expenses, were also not allowed, although difficult to detect.

A firm had an alternative to filing for a price increase on a four-digit
SIC basis; this was to enter into a Term Limited Pricing Agreement (TLP).
The TLP was an agreement between the Price Commission and the firm
for one year, whereby the firm would not raise its average price level
by more than 1.8 percent with a maximum of 6 percent on any particular
product.* This had to be cost-justified under the above definition. In
return the firm was not required to prenotify each time it adjusted a
price.

The so-called "second line of defense" was the profit margin limitation. A firm was not allowed to raise its prices if its profit margin
was greater than the average of the best two out of three fiscal years
prior to the control program (that is, fiscal years ending prior to August
14, 1971). For most firms this was the average of the years 1968 and
1969, which relative to 1971 were quite good for margins. If a firm
raised no prices, it was not subject to the profit margin limit. If it
did, and went over the profit margin limitation, the penalty was only
the dollar amount over the limit or the revenue gleaned from the price
increases, whichever was less. Firms entering TLP agreements were
also subject to the profit margin limitation.

---

*Initially 2 percent with no maximums on any given product.

The first observation is that the TLP agreement, being applicable to all firms, was an abbrogation of controls for many firms. In chemicals, for example, prices typically do not rise by 1.8 percent, particularly during an expansion. Electrical machinery, SIC 36, is another example.

The third observation is that the profit margin is primarily a function of output. In reviewing the impact of prices and costs on margins, it would tend to discourage increased production or encourage creative accounting if effective. In point of fact, most industries were far below the 1968-69 average profit margin at the beginning of Phase II, except for food processing, which has a nearly constant profit margin. In this industry the margin limit could have been predicted to have a fairly capricious effect.

The wage equations clearly add further evidence that the U.S. economy is a complicated one. Where if there is a long-run convex trade-off between unemployment and inflation, the economy is subject to change as various institutional and technological factors change over time. Further, its exact position at any point in time depends upon the form stimulative policy takes. However, there remains, in a general sense, an unemployment-inflation tradeoff, one that is not destroyed over time by attempting to maintain a lower level of unemployment and higher rate of inflation. These observations are further complicated by the timing effects and changes in the form of wage increases that are induced by trade unions.[10]

The guideposts of the Kennedy-Johnson years show up with a significantly negative impact in 13 of the 16 manufacturing industries. Combining these bits of information, one would expect incomes policies to work in the sense of improving the Phillips tradeoff, but that such policies would have to be flexible to allow for different conditions in the various sectors of the economy. Thus fashioned, it may take such policies some time to show up in aggregate data.

It is our view that the institution of the price and wage control program generated an expectation of price stability that was generally complied with in a voluntary manner, but in sectors that were not subject to strict enforcement. The price rules as they applied to manufacturing were naive, and the consequences, accordingly, were not impressive in the concentrated industries. The lack of flexibility, again particularly on the price side, caused by lack of effective controls led to distortions in areas where shortages developed (hides and lumber). The position established by the control program was, therefore, clearly untenable, and while in terms of consumer prices Phase II was a short-run success, it was, in the longer view of things, a failure in terms of promulgating and enforcing effective controls.

APPENDIX

All variables except for the unemployment rate, industry pretax profits, and the layoff rate for all manufacturing are four-quarter percentage rates of change, weighted averages of these rates of change, or lagged values of rates of change. An "F" affixed to the end variable name indicates the four-quarter rate of change; an "FWA" indicates a weighted average of rates formed for a variable X as follows:

$$XFWA = (.4*XF + .3*XF(-1) + .2*XF(-2) + .1*XF(-3)$$

Given the above conventions, the following is a list of all variables used in the analysis. Since the digital element of the variable name indicates the SIC industry to which it pertains, the list includes only the separate types of variables without listing the variables for each industry.

PQ	Industry of output price
PM	Profit margin before federal income taxes
AHE[	Index of average hourly earnings for production workers adjusted for overtime and interindustry shifts
AHE	Index of average hourly earnings without adjustment for overtime and interindustry shifts
PIN	Index of input price
CPI	Consumer Price Index for all items
EP	Employment of production workers
GDP	Guidepost dummy variable with constructed values from 62:1 to 67:3 and zero otherwise
INV%SC	Inventories as a percent of sales
JG%MHM	Output per man-hour for all manufacturing
ZADP%EG	Pretax profits plus depreciation as a percent of stockholders equity
RMAA	Moody's Aaa corporate bond rate
JFRB	Index of industrial production
1/U	Inverse of the civilian unemployment rate
CNCS58	Consumption expenditures on apparel in 1958 dollars
LAYOFF	Layoff rate for all manufacturing per 100 employees seasonally adjusted
INV%S	Inventories as percent of shipments
CPIEXP=	$\sum_{i=0}^{7}$ CPIF(-i)-.2 if positive i=0; otherwise CPIEXP = 0
UCAPFRB	Index of capacity utilization
DP	Depreciation
ESP=	1 in 1971:3-1972:4; otherwise ESP = 0

NOTES

1. Otto Eckstein and David Wyss, "Industry Price Equations, " The Econometrics of Price Determination/Conference (Washington, D. C.: Board of Governors, Federal Reserve System, 1972).

2. D. Heien and J. Popkin, "Price Determination and Cost of Living Measures in a Disaggregated Model of the U. S. Economy." The Econometrics of Price Determination/Conference (Washington, D. C.: Board of Governors, Federal Reserve System, 1972).

3. The indexes of output and input prices were constructed using procedures established by Eckstein and Wyss, op. cit.

4. See R. J. Barro, "A Theory of Monopolistic Price Adjustment, " Review of Economic Studies 39 (January 1972): 17-26, for a discussion of the cost of changing prices on the determination of the rate of price adjustment.

5. A. W. Phillips, "The Relationship between Unemployment and the Rate of Change of Money Wage Rates in the United Kingdom, 1861-1957, " Economica, new series, 25, no. 100 (November 1958): 283-99; R. G. Lipsey, "The Relation Between Unemployment and the Rate of Change in Money Wages Rates in the U. S., 1862-1957: A Further Analysis, " Economica new series 27 no. 105 (February 1960): 1-31; Otto Eckstein and Thomas A. Wilson, "The Determination of Money Wages in American Industry, " Quarterly Journal of Economics 86 (August 1962): 379-414; C. Schultze and J. Tryon, "Prices and Wages, " Brookings Quarterly Econometric Model of the United States (Chicago: Rand McNally 1965); Edwin Kuh, "A Productivity Theory of Wage Levels—An Alternative to the Phillips Curve, " Review of Economic Studies (October 1967), pp. 333-60; Milton Friedman, "The Role of Monetary Policy, " American Economic Review 58 (March 1968): 1-17. G. A. Akerlof, "Relative Wages and the Rate of Inflation, " Quarterly Journal of Economics, 83 (August 1969): 353-74; Edmund S. Phelps, Armon A. Alchain, Charles C. Holt, Dale T. Mortensen, G. C. Archibald, Robert E. Lucas Jr., Leonard Rapping, Sidney G. Winter, Jr., John P. Gould, Donald F. Gordon, Allan Hynis, Donald A. Nichols, Paul T. Taubman, Maurice Wilkinson, The Microeconomic Foundations of Employment and Inflation Theory (New York: W. W. Norton and Co., 1970).

6. As argued, for example, in Phillips, op. cit.; Lipsey, op. cit.; Kuh, op. cit.; Akerlof, op cit.; and Arthur Okun, "Upward Mobility in a High Pressure Economy, " Brookings Papers on Economic Activity, 1 (1973), pp. 207-52.

7. This position has been espoused in Friedman, op cit., and Phelps, et al., op. cit. A review of this literature is found in Albert Rees, Wage-Price Policy, (New York: General Learning Corporation, 1971).

8. op. cit.

9. Some general industry studies are Eckstein and Wilson, op. citl; and M. L. Wachter, "Relative Wage Equations for U. S. Manufacturing Industries, " Review of Economics and Statistics 52 (November 1970): 405-10.

10. This has been documented by Charles C. Holt "Job Search, Phillips Wage Relation and Union Influence, Theory and Evidence" in E. S. Phelps, pp. 224-256. op. cit.; O. C. Ashenfelter, G. E. Johnson, and J. H. Pencavel, "Trade Unions and the Rate of Change of Money Wages in the United States Manufacturing Industry, " Review of Economic Studies, 39 (April 1, 1972): 27-54; and Daniel S. Hammermesh, "Market Power and Wage Inflation, " Southern Economic Journal (October 1972), pp. 204-12, among others.

CHAPTER

8

AN ANALYSIS OF
THE ECONOMIC
STABILIZATION
PROGRAM THROUGH
STAGES OF PROCESSING
Paul H. Earl

The United States economy experienced nearly three years of price controls from August 1971 until the dismantling of the Economic Stabilization Program in April 1974. The intensity and coverage of the controls on prices and wages varied widely during the program, and its effect on price behavior continues to be the center of much debate, as does the viability of any controls program and the long-run effect of price controls on capacity and incentive to expand.

This chapter represents a disaggregate analysis of the impact on price behavior of the Economic Stabilization Program from the fourth quarter of 1971 through the first quarter of 1974. The framework for the analysis is a price model by stages of processing, which is explained in the next section and in the appendix. The sectoral nature of this model enables a more precise analysis of controls to be made relative to the many aggregate studies.[1] Difficulties in isolating the impact of price controls and methods of analysis are discussed in the following section. The last sections contain findings and summary comments.

FRAMEWORK FOR THE ANALYSIS

The stages-of-processing model utilized in this study is a sectoral input-output depiction of price behavior in the U.S. economy. Figure 8.1 displays the stages-of-processing structure within each sector of the economy. Price relationships are analyzed at each level of production and are linked to price behavior at other stages of processing and in other sectors. The levels of production included are crude materials, intermediate materials, finished goods, and retail products. These levels, where appropriate, are examined for the durable goods, nondurable goods less food and fuel, food, energy, services,

117

FIGURE 8.1

Flow Chart: Stages-of-Processing Price Model

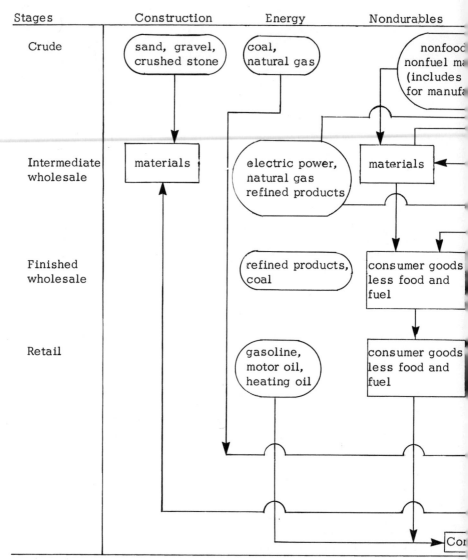

Note: Squares represent variables endogenous to the model; circles re
also, to form aggregates at each of the four stages.
Source: Compiled by the author.

les   Other   Services   Food

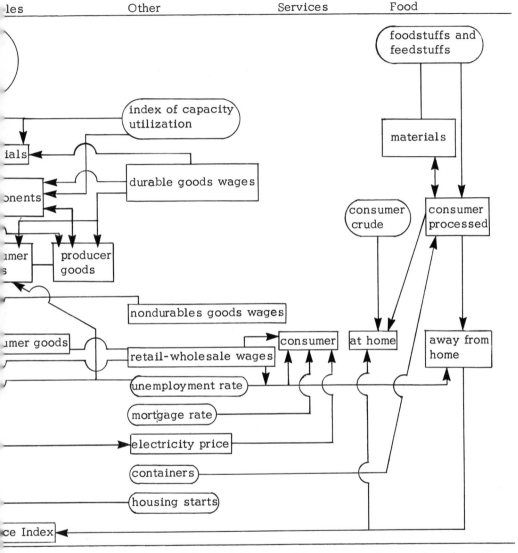

ariables exogenous to the model. Variables combine across stages of production,

118

WAGE AND PRICE CONTROLS

and construction sectors. The Bureau of Labor Statistics wholesale prices by stages of processing, other selected wholesale prices, and sectoral consumer price indexes comprise the core of the price data base from which the model is built.

The microeconomic basis for each of the price equations in the model lies in the theories of short-run profit maximization, market disequilibrium adjustment, and target rate of return. The short-run profit maximization theory uses Equation 1 below as its foundation, with the price required for profit maximization given in Equation 2.

1. $PR = PQ - AHE^{*}Q^{*}(1/PP) - PIN^{*}MAT^{*}Q$

Where PR = profits; P = price; Q = output; AHE = average hourly earnings; PP = productivity ($=Q/H$ where H = total man-hours); PIN = material prices; and MAT = materials consumed per unit of output

2. $P = AHE^{*}(1/PP) + PIN^{*}MAT$

If changes in marginal cost are assumed equal to changes in unit variable costs, that is, material and labor, then Equation 3 can be derived from Equation 2.

3. $\Delta P = \Delta AHE^{*}(1/PP) + \Delta(1/PP)^{*}AHE + \Delta PIN^{*}MAT + \Delta MAT^{*}PIN$

The market disequilibrium adjustment is depicted in Equation 4 below.

4. $\Delta P = f(QD - QS)$

Where QD = quantity demanded; QS = quantity supplied
Prices adjust to equilibrium based on imbalances that exist between the demand for and supply of a product.

The target return theory is a long-run theory of price behavior in which prices depend on factor prices, including capital, and long-run productivity. The price equation, assuming again that changes in marginal costs equal changes in unit costs, is given in Equation 5.

5. $\Delta P = \Delta AHE^{*}(H/QN) + \Delta(H/QN)^{*}AHE + \Delta PIN^{*}(MATN)$
     $+ \Delta MATN^{*}PIN + \Delta r^{*}KN + \Delta KN^{*}r$

Where QN = normalized, long-run output levels; MATN = materials consumed per unit of normalized output; r = target rate of return on capital; KN = capital per unit of normalized output

A number of factors combine to make the empirical explanation of price behavior using Equations 3, 4, or 5 difficult, including the complexity of the pricing mechanism, difficulties in aggregation and application of micro theories to macro data, and a lack of compatibility of theory and available data. Instead, a hybrid of the theories is the most common specification utilized in explaining price behavior. [2] This mix of theories enables one to ascertain the degree to which changes in cost and market conditions affect price movements.

The specifications for price equations are therefore hybrids of the theories contained in Equations 3 and 4. Average hourly earnings (AHE) are represented by indexes, where appropriate, for workers in retail and wholesale, durable goods, and nondurable goods industries. Material prices (PIN) at each processing stage are represented by the output prices from the previous stage in the production process. These material prices include energy costs, which are exogenous, as well as material costs, as indicated in the flow chart. The material prices represent the driving forces in the price movements of each sector, since changes in prices at lower processing stages subsequently feed into prices at higher stages. Market disequilibrium measures include the unemployment rate, the index of capacity utilization in major materials industries, and the number of housing starts.

Productivity measures were constructed and tested, but rejected because of a lack of data reliability. However, productivity is included implicitly, with its effect represented in the constant terms, consistent with the neoclassical view. The target-rate-of-return concept was tested, using measures such as long-term bond rates and profits-sales or profit-equity ratios. These measures were found less significant than cost and market indicators, due primarily to the lack of compatibility of target-return measures with price variables at such a high level of aggregation.

Structural specifications and timing relationships of the cost and market measures vary among sectors and through stages of processing. Lag structures representing the timing relationships between each factor in the pricing process and the final prices were carefully specified, utilizing a priori knowledge and statistical techniques. The resulting structural specification indicate a greater importance of market measures at the higher processing stages. Also, the lag structures cover a longer interval in durable goods than in other sectors. Furthermore, the lags in the price feed-through process are much shorter and the importance of market measures considerably less in the food sector.

Quarterly seasonally-adjusted data, generally available from 1960 through 1974:1, are utilized to estimate this model. All of the analysis is performed on data expressed in percent-of-change form at annual rates. Statistical summary results for the behavioral equations in the model, along with actual specifications and variable definitions, are given in the appendix.

METHODOLOGY

Isolating the precise impact of a selected economic condition or policy is difficult because of both the continual flux in other economic factors during the same period and the interrelationships (that is, lack of independence) among most policies and conditions in the economy. Over the 1971:4-1974:1 period the United States also experienced considerably higher rates of increase in its monetary base, bank credit, and money stock than in the previous decade, as well as substantially higher import prices. Therefore certain forms of econometric analysis might conclude erroneously that the ESP had an insignificant impact on dampening inflation rates if the impacts of these other factors, both of which contribute to an acceleration in inflation, were greater. Disaggregate analysis of the type presented in this paper[3] tends to reduce the probability of drawing inaccurate conclusions, since the impact of changes in monetary policy is much less significant on individual product prices than it is on aggregate prices. Other problems involved in ascertaining the impact of the ESP on price behavior include (1) problems in fitting the timing of the initiation of ESP phases to quarterly data; and (2) the varying degrees of control over the period. These problems can best be handled by a careful construction of dummy variables.

The methods of analysis utilized in this research are dummy variable testing and ex post simulations. Two types of dummy variables are constructed and tested, constant-shift and price-relation twist. The constant-shift dummies are typical of most analyses of price controls. Individual dummies are formed for each of the phases as well as one for the entire controls period as follows:

Constant-Shift Dummy		Values	Dates of Phase
All	1	1971:4-1974:1	August 15, 1971 to
	0	otherwise	April 20, 1974
Phase I	1	1971:4	August 15, 1971 to
	0	otherwise	November 15, 1971
Phase 2	1	1972:1-1972:4	November 16, 1971 to
	0	otherwise	January 10, 1973
Phase 3 (includes second freeze)	1	1973:1-1973:2	January 11, 1973 to
	0	otherwise	July 17, 1973
Phase 4	1	1973:3-1974:1	July 18, 1973 to
	0	otherwise	April 30, 1974

The lack of exact compatability between the start-up dates of the phases and of the quarters of the year is evident. Therefore each of the dummy variables, although mainly representing a particular phase, also reflects the effects of the bordering phases. The third quarter of 1971 is not considered to be part of the controls period, since two of its three months of price data (July and August) were collected prior to the imposition of the freeze.

Also tested are dummies, termed price-relation twists, constructed to test whether different relationships between input and output price variables existed before controls than during controls. This type of dummy permits the analysis of uneven impacts of controls through the stages of processing within a sector. The constant-shift dummies, on the other hand, are most useful in controls effectiveness comparisons across sectors. The price-relation shift dummies are constructed to be equal to the input price variable over the 1971:4-1974:1 period and zero otherwise. Price-relation twist dummies have not been constructed for the individual phases of the ESP; if they had been, they would have permitted further analysis of uneven impacts, phase by phase.

For each behavioral relationship, four regressions were estimated, using dummy variables to test the impact of the ESP. These include (1) constant-shift dummies for each phase; (2) one constant-shift dummy for the entire ESP; (3) price-relation twist with the dummies for each phase, and (4) price-relation twist with the dummy for the entire ESP. Results are depicted in detail in Tables 8.1 through 8.4 inclusive. Constant-shift dummies that are negative and significant indicate a significant dampening in inflation rates during their periods of coverage. The price-relation twist dummies do not have an expected directional effect, since a given output-input price relation can be widened or narrowed depending on the relative impact and coverage of controls on each price.

The second method of analysis utilized is that of ex post simulations over the controls period. The behavioral equations in the stages-of-processing price model, given in the appendix, are reestimated through 1971:3 for results that are not affected by the data during the period of ESP. Data during this latter period could bias regression results if temporary structural changes in relationships among variables occurred. If, on the other hand, a permanent shift in relatioships took place during controls, the data prior to 1971:4 would not be relevant among the estimation intervals. Two versions of the stages-of-processing model can be simulated over the 1971:4-1974:1 period; one based on equations estimated on data through 1974:1 ("with controls") and the other through 1971:3 ("without controls"). The "with controls" solution is the tracking of the actual model over the ESP period. The "without controls" is a tracking of price movements, given that the ESP did not occur. If the partial effects of different variables on one another over the two periods of estimation were the same, then these two solutions would be equivalent.

However, this is not the case presently, which indicates some shift in relationships during the ESP.

The simulation results in the next section must be evaluated in light of the following limitations. First, exogenous prices in the model are assumed at their observed values for the simulations. Most of the exogenous prices are commodity prices that accelerated in their rates of increase during 1973:1-1974:1. Because of this limitation the findings for the total wholesale and consumer price indexes are not discussed. Second, all nonprice variables, including wages, are assumed to exhibit their actual behavior over the period. The short-run effect of the ESP on employment, capacity expansion, and investment appeared to be minimal. Also, actual wage increases during the ESP were generally under the targeted maximums that were set.

FINDINGS

The results from the dummy variable analysis and simulation analyses are given in Tables 8.1 through 8.6. These results are discussed sector by sector in this section. Tables 8.1, 8.2, 8.3, and 8.4 contain the dummy variable analysis, and Tables 8.5 and 8.6 give the price levels and annual rates of change for the simulations.

Food. The only constant-shift dummies that are significant are the individual phase dummies in the retail equation for restaurant meal prices (see Table 8.1). Many of the dummy variables in the other food (that is, unprocessed food such as fresh fruits and vegetables) and crude foodstuffs and feedstuffs, which are both regressors in selected equations, were uncontrolled during the ESP. This, coupled with the rapid commodity inflation during 1973 and 1974, exerted pressure on the profit margins of processed food categories, which were controlled.

The significant twist dummies in the food price equations at various stages of processing are generally positive in effect. When combined with the positive coefficients relating input and output prices in these relationships, the net effect is to indicate a higher precent of increase in a higher stage of processing price during controls than prior to controls, given the same 1 percent increase in the price at the next lower stage of processing. The one exception to this behavior is the relationship between processed food (at wholesale), and crude foodstuffs and feedstuffs. Since the latter were uncontrolled while the former were controlled, this result is not surprising.

The ex post simulation results generally support the above findings of only minor effects of controls on food prices (see Tables 8.5 and 8.6). For retail food prices both at home and at restaurants, the annual inflation rates are an average of 2 percent less without controls, with

TABLE 8.1

Food Sector, Dummy Variable Analysis of Price Controls

| | Constant Effects: Phases | | | | | Twist |
	I	II	III	IV	All	Effect
Retail						
At home						
1	+	-	+	+		
2					+	
3	+	+	+	+		+, -
4				-		+, -
Restaurant						
1	-	+	+	+		
2					+	
3	-2.57	-2.66	-5.16	-6.74		.555
4					+	.336
Wholesale						
Processed						
1	+	-	-	+		
2					+	
3	+	-	+	+		-, -
4					+	.122, -.155
Materials						
for food						
manufacturing						
1	-	-	+	+		
2					+	
3	-	+	+	+		+, -
4				-		+, .524

Note: Where significant at $\alpha = .05$, coefficient values are given,
1, 2, 3, 4 refer to dummy variable tests see p. 122.

the gap widening during Phases 3 and 4. Note that both of these price series contain unprocessed items the prices of which were uncontrolled. Intermediate materials for food manufacturing have annual price increases 3 to 18 percent lower in the no-controls solution than with controls. Processed food at wholesale exhibits nearly the same inflation rates in both the presence and absence of controls.

Durables. Based on the dummy variable analysis, the ESP did not exert any significant impact on consumer durable goods prices at both the final wholesale and the retail stages of processing (see Table 8.2).

TABLE 8.2

Durable Goods Sector,
Dummy Variable Analysis of Price Controls

	Constant Effects: Phases					Twist
	1	2	3	4	All	Effect
Retail						
Consumer						
1	-	+	+	ı		
2					+	
3	-	+	+	+		-
4					+	-
Final wholesale						
Consumer						
1	+	-	+	-		
2					+	
3	+	-	+	-		+
4				-		+
Producer						
1	-2.19	-.98	+	-		
2					-	
3	-3.48	-1.96	-	-		+
4				-		+
Intermediate						
wholesale						
Components						
1	-	-	-	-		
2					-	
3	-	+	-	-		-
4					+	-.263
Materials						
1	-	-4.94	-	-8.94		
2					-3.15	
3	+	+	+	+		-.480
4				-		-.190

Note: Where significant at $\alpha = .05$, coefficient values are given. 1, 2, 3, 4 refer to dummy variable tests, see p. 122.

The constant-shift dummies indicate a significant dampening effect of Phase I and II on the price of producer finished goods, with Phase I having the greatest effect. The gradual decontrol of selected durable products and materials during Phases III and IV, with the prime examples being ferrous and nonferrous scrap, increased the impact of allowable cost pass-throughs in this sector; as a result, price controls did not have a significant impact during this period. The entire ESP had a significant slowing effect on the rate of increase in intermediate durable materials prices, by about 3 percent (annual rate) per quarter below what they would otherwise have been. This suppression of price increases and the accompanying squeeze on profit margins has surfaced since decontrol as rapid increases in the prices of most ferrous and nonferrous materials. Less pass-through of price increases at the lower stages of processing is indicated by the significant negative price-relation twist dummy variables.

The results from the simulation analysis in Tables 8.5 and 8.6 corroborate the above findings. Consumer goods prices at retail and final wholesale are slightly lower in the no-controls solution during the ESP, with the gap widening during Phases III and IV. Producer finished goods and intermediate durable components both increase at nearly 2 percent (annual rate) more per quarter assuming no price controls. Intermediate materials for durable manufacturing exhibit higher inflation rates under the no-controls simulation through 1973:3, but lower rates during the final two quarters. The rapid commodity inflation in many items included in crude, nonfood, nonfuel materials for manufacturing during 1973 and 1974:1 makes the effects of the ESP on intermediate durable materials difficult to ascertain.

Nondurables less Food and Fuel. The results in Table 8.3 show nearly no impact of the ESP on dampening inflation in nondurable goods less food and fuel. With the exception of the intermediate materials price equation, all constant-shift dummies have negative coefficients; however, their effects are insignificant. All constant-shift dummies in the intermediate materials price equation also indicate insignificant effects of the ESP but in a positive direction. This result can be partly attributed to the allowable pass-through of price increases in hides, which were uncontrolled during the ESP; the true relationship of hides to leather is not reflected in this equation. The simulation results, of Tables 8.5 and 8.6 indicate lower inflation rates over the 1971:4-1974:1 period in the absence of price controls for both final goods and intermediate materials at wholesale. At retail the with- and without-controls simulations yield nearly identical results through Phase II; however, the without-controls simulation yields lower inflation rates through Phases III and IV.

Other Sectors. No dummy variables in Table 8.4 are significant in either the services or construction materials price equations. However, the ex post simulation results (Tables 8.5 and 8.6) indicate that the without-controls solution has lower inflation rates than the with-controls solution in the services sector through all of the ESP, and in construction materials through Phase II.

TABLE 8. 3

Nondurables less Food and Fuel,
Dummy Variable Analysis of Price Controls

| | Constant Effects: Phases | | | | | Twist |
	1	2	3	4	All	Effect
Retail						
1	-	-	-	-		
2					-	
3	-	-	-	- 2. 62		+
4					-	+
Final wholesale						
1	-	-	-	-		
2					-	
3	-	-	-	-		+
4					-	+
Intermediate wholesale						
1	+	+	+	+		
2					+	
3	+	+	+	+		-
4					+	+. 217

Note: Where significant at α = . 05, coefficient values are given.
1, 2, 3, 4, refer to dummy variable tests, see p. 122.

SUMMARY

The results discussed in the previous section do not allow clear
conclusions to be drawn regarding the effectiveness of the Economic
Stabilization Program in dampening inflation. The two econometric
approaches have difficulties in measuring the precise impact of price
controls. In the case of the dummy variable method, other influences
on prices during the controls period that are not explicitly included in
the relationship might also have their effects represented by the dummies.
For the ex post simulation method, the assumption that controls had no
influence on nonprice factors in the behavioral relationships could be
questioned. Nonetheless, certain conclusions do emerge. Table 8.7
contains the annual rates of increase for the stages-of-processing
prices during each of the phases of the ESP, assuming with and without
controls, as well as for the period immediately preceding controls.

TABLE 8.4

Services and Construction Materials,
Dummy Variable Analysis of Price Controls

| | Constant Effects: Phases | | | | | Twist |
	1	2	3	4	All	Effect
Services						
1	-	-	-	+		
3					+	
Construction materials						
1	-	-	+	-		
2					-	
3	-	-	+	-		+
4					-	+

Note: Where significant at $\alpha = .05$, coefficient values are given.
1, 2, 3, 4 refer to dummy variable tests, see p. 122.

First, the results of the analysis indicate a significant impact of
the ESP in reducing inflation rates below those in a without-controls
economy for services, producer durable goods, intermediate durable
materials, and construction materials. Services prices increase at
annual rates considerably below the 6.2 rate of the 1970:1-1971:3
period through Phase III, with the controls solution considerably below
the without-controls solution for Phases II through IV. Similar results
are evident for producer durable goods, including a considerable dampening of inflation during Phase I. In the cases of durable and construction materials, the impact of the ESP lessens considerably during Phases
III and IV. This finding is consistent with the closer proximity of these
materials to the rampant commodity inflation during that period. Even
though the inflation rates are dampened, they are generally well above
the target rate of 2.5 percent set by the Administration.

Second, the results clearly indicate an acceleration in the rates
of inflation in stages-of-processing prices during 1973 and 1974. Attri-
buting this acceleration to the presence of controls is nonsense; however, the loose nature of the controls administrative machinery relative
to that during Phases I and II certainly may have contributed to a reduction in effectiveness in the later phases. More importantly, price
controls were not designed to reduce the commodity-based inflation of
the 1973-74 period. Therefore, less distortions of both real and price
behavior may have resulted in a no-controls economy.

Third, this analysis provides information that should be examined
when considering the reimposition of price controls. Controls appear

TABLE 8.5

Summary: Prices by Stages of Processing
(1967 levels = 1.0)

	1971:4	1972:1	1972:2	1972:3	1972:4	1973:1	1973:2	1973:3	1973:4	1974:1
RETAIL										
Food	1.201	1.218	1.224	1.238	1.261	1.316	1.378	1.454	1.507	1.571
With controls	1.200	1.217	1.231	1.257	1.291	1.338	1.406	1.481	1.530	1.563
Without controls	1.200	1.216	1.228	1.250	1.280	1.321	1.378	1.440	1.478	1.502
Food at home	1.180	1.199	1.202	1.218	1.243	1.307	1.377	1.461	1.512	1.582
With controls	1.178	1.196	1.210	1.238	1.276	1.329	1.406	1.489	1.539	1.570
Without controls	1.178	1.195	1.207	1.232	1.266	1.313	1.379	1.450	1.491	1.515
Food away from home	1.280	1.291	1.305	1.318	1.332	1.350	1.386	1.427	1.493	1.529
With controls	1.283	1.296	1.312	1.328	1.347	1.371	1.406	1.449	1.501	1.536
Without controls	1.281	1.293	1.306	1.319	1.333	1.350	1.373	1.400	1.431	1.455
Durables	1.169	1.176	1.183	1.198	1.199	1.204	1.216	1.226	1.230	1.241
With controls	1.174	1.184	1.190	1.193	1.196	1.202	1.206	1.213	1.221	1.237
Without controls	1.174	1.183	1.188	1.189	1.191	1.195	1.199	1.205	1.212	1.228
Nondurables less food and fuel	1.198	1.207	1.215	1.219	1.228	1.234	1.250	1.258	1.272	1.295
With controls	1.197	1.206	1.213	1.222	1.231	1.239	1.252	1.267	1.286	1.306
Without controls	1.199	1.207	1.215	1.224	1.233	1.241	1.253	1.265	1.278	1.290
Services	1.303	1.318	1.327	1.338	1.350	1.362	1.376	1.394	1.430	1.459
With controls	1.306	1.320	1.331	1.342	1.353	1.364	1.378	1.394	1.413	1.444
Without controls	1.305	1.319	1.329	1.342	1.353	1.364	1.382	1.402	1.428	1.486

128

WHOLESALE

Processed food	1.177	1.195	1.200	1.220	1.256	1.332	1.394	1.503	1.528	1.588
With controls	1.173	1.192	1.210	1.245	1.286	1.360	1.438	1.542	1.538	1.583
Without controls	1.174	1.194	1.212	1.248	1.291	1.369	1.450	1.559	1.546	1.590
Consumer durables	1.116	1.127	1.132	1.141	1.130	1.138	1.156	1.165	1.172	1.199
With controls	1.113	1.123	1.128	1.135	1.138	1.146	1.154	1.163	1.177	1.203
Without controls	1.114	1.121	1.125	1.129	1.132	1.138	1.145	1.153	1.164	1.184
Producer durables	1.173	1.184	1.194	1.200	1.201	1.209	1.229	1.241	1.260	1.292
With controls	1.178	1.186	1.194	1.204	1.212	1.220	1.231	1.246	1.267	1.301
Without controls	1.182	1.195	1.207	1.221	1.233	1.246	1.263	1.285	1.313	1.352
Nondurables less food and fuel	1.132	1.138	1.148	1.151	1.158	1.168	1.183	1.186	1.215	1.252
With controls	1.134	1.141	1.150	1.157	1.163	1.174	1.189	1.208	1.228	1.255
Without controls	1.134	1.140	1.149	1.154	1.159	1.167	1.176	1.186	1.197	1.202
Food materials	1.178	1.183	1.186	1.194	1.234	1.307	1.393	1.539	1.605	1.805
With controls	1.190	1.212	1.238	1.277	1.326	1.415	1.522	1.669	1.718	1.787
Without controls	1.186	1.202	1.219	1.246	1.278	1.335	1.397	1.481	1.498	1.536
Durable components	1.156	1.164	1.175	1.180	1.182	1.191	1.208	1.218	1.239	1.277
With controls	1.157	1.165	1.174	1.184	1.192	1.200	1.213	1.232	1.256	1.292
Without controls	1.164	1.175	1.185	1.196	1.208	1.222	1.243	1.269	1.299	1.338
Durable materials	1.219	1.227	1.230	1.241	1.255	1.284	1.327	1.344	1.395	1.487
With controls	1.217	1.232	1.250	1.272	1.289	1.314	1.352	1.396	1.448	1.525
Without controls	1.225	1.240	1.264	1.287	1.307	1.338	1.379	1.429	1.481	1.514
Nondurables less food and fuel	1.065	1.075	1.086	1.098	1.119	1.142	1.191	1.234	1.275	1.365
With controls	1.067	1.078	1.099	1.112	1.125	1.151	1.195	1.250	1.306	1.356
Without controls	1.063	1.067	1.077	1.084	1.090	1.103	1.122	1.145	1.167	1.187
Construction materials	1.228	1.240	1.252	1.269	1.287	1.313	1.369	1.372	1.415	1.478
With controls	1.236	1.253	1.275	1.299	1.326	1.352	1.384	1.409	1.434	1.493
Without controls	1.246	1.269	1.299	1.328	1.364	1.399	1.432	1.456	1.467	1.473

TABLE 8.6

Summary: Prices by Stages of Processing, by Annual Rates of Change

RETAIL	1971:4	1972:1	1972:2	1972:3	1972:4	1973:1	1973:2	1973:3	1973:4	1974:1
Food	3.5	6.0	1.8	4.9	7.6	18.5	20.2	24.1	15.4	17.9
With controls	3.4	5.8	4.7	8.4	11.4	15.5	21.7	23.1	14.1	8.7
Without controls	3.3	5.4	4.2	7.3	9.9	13.4	18.4	19.3	11.1	6.6
Food at home	3.5	6.8	0.9	5.5	8.5	22.1	23.1	27.0	14.7	19.6
With controls	2.9	6.3	4.7	9.5	13.0	17.8	25.0	26.0	14.0	8.4
Without controls	2.9	5.8	4.2	8.3	11.5	15.8	21.7	22.4	11.6	6.6
Food away from home	3.3	3.5	4.3	4.1	4.2	5.6	11.1	12.4	19.7	9.9
With controls	4.1	4.1	4.9	5.0	5.8	7.5	10.6	12.8	14.9	9.8
Without controls	3.6	3.7	4.0	4.1	4.4	5.3	6.9	8.0	9.2	6.7
Durables	-0.3	2.2	2.5	5.1	0.5	1.6	4.1	3.3	1.2	3.7
With controls	1.3	3.4	2.2	0.9	1.0	1.9	1.5	2.2	2.8	5.4
Without controls	1.2	3.1	1.8	0.3	0.6	1.5	1.2	2.0	2.5	5.2
Nondurables less food and fuel	2.1	2.9	2.8	1.2	3.0	2.1	5.3	2.7	4.4	7.3
With controls	1.9	2.8	2.4	2.9	3.0	2.9	4.3	4.9	5.9	6.6
Without controls	2.3	3.0	2.6	2.9	3.0	2.8	3.7	3.8	4.2	3.9
Services	3.1	4.7	2.9	3.3	3.5	3.6	4.3	5.3	10.7	8.3
With controls	4.1	4.3	3.3	3.5	3.2	3.4	4.1	4.6	5.7	9.0
Without controls	3.9	4.1	3.3	3.9	3.2	3.2	5.4	6.1	7.4	17.2

Processed Food	9.2	6.6	1.5	6.9	12.3	26.7	20.1	34.8	6.8	16.8
With controls	7.7	6.6	6.3	12.0	14.0	25.0	24.9	32.5	-1.0	12.0
Without controls	8.3	6.9	6.0	12.6	14.6	26.5	25.6	33.8	-3.4	11.9
Consumer durables	1.0	4.3	1.5	3.2	-3.7	2.9	6.5	3.2	2.3	9.8
With controls	0.1	3.4	2.0	2.3	1.0	2.9	2.9	3.2	4.8	9.1
Without controls	0.5	2.4	1.4	1.6	0.8	2.2	2.5	2.7	3.9	7.1
Producer Durables	0.6	3.8	3.4	2.1	0.1	2.7	6.8	4.0	6.2	10.8
With controls	2.1	2.7	2.9	3.4	2.8	2.6	3.7	4.9	6.9	11.3
Without controls	3.6	4.5	4.1	4.5	4.0	4.3	5.8	7.1	8.8	12.7
Nondurables less food and fuel	0.6	2.1	3.4	1.2	2.6	3.5	5.2	1.0	9.9	12.9
With controls	1.2	2.5	3.3	2.4	2.2	3.6	5.4	6.3	7.0	9.1
Without controls	1.5	2.0	3.0	1.7	1.9	2.7	3.1	3.6	3.5	1.7
Food materials	2.8	1.8	1.2	2.5	14.1	25.8	28.9	49.3	18.2	60.2
With controls	7.4	7.4	8.8	13.2	16.4	29.8	33.6	44.6	12.5	16.9
Without controls	5.8	5.5	5.8	9.1	10.9	18.9	20.1	26.2	4.8	10.4
Durable Components	1.5	2.9	3.9	1.5	0.9	2.8	5.9	3.4	7.0	13.1
With controls	1.8	2.6	3.1	3.5	2.8	2.8	4.3	6.4	8.2	11.9
Without controls	4.3	3.7	3.6	3.9	3.8	4.8	7.1	8.6	10.0	12.4
Durable materials	3.7	2.6	0.9	3.7	4.5	9.7	14.0	5.1	16.1	29.3
With controls	3.0	4.8	6.2	7.0	5.5	8.0	12.0	13.7	16.0	23.0
Without controls	5.8	5.0	7.8	7.4	6.4	9.8	12.8	15.5	15.4	9.0
Nondurables less food and fuel	2.0	3.9	4.3	4.1	7.9	8.8	18.0	15.2	14.1	31.4
With controls	2.9	4.3	7.7	4.8	4.8	9.9	15.9	19.9	19.1	16.3
Without controls	1.2	1.6	3.8	2.5	2.5	4.7	7.0	8.4	8.1	7.0
Construction materials	3.3	4.1	3.9	5.5	5.8	8.3	18.4	0.6	13.4	19.0
With controls	6.0	5.6	7.2	7.9	8.4	8.3	9.7	7.5	7.4	17.5
Without controls	9.6	7.4	9.8	9.4	11.3	10.9	9.7	6.7	3.2	1.5

TABLE 8.7

Price Movements with and without Controls, by Annual Rates of Change

Sectors	1970:1-1971:3	Phase 1 with	Phase 1 without	Phase 2 with	Phase 2 without	Phase 3 with	Phase 3 without	Phase 4 with	Phase 4 without
Retail									
Food	2.9	3.4	3.3	9.9	8.7	22.4	18.8	11.4	8.8
Food at home	2.1	2.9	2.9	11.1	9.9	25.5	22.1	11.1	9.1
Food away from home	5.6	4.1	3.6	5.8	4.4	11.7	7.5	12.3	7.9
Durables	4.6	1.3	1.2	1.5	1.1	1.8	1.6	4.1	3.9
Nondurables less food and fuel	3.8	1.9	2.3	2.8	2.8	4.1	3.8	6.3	4.1
Services	6.2	4.1	3.9	3.4	3.4	4.4	5.7	7.3	12.2
Wholesale									
Processed Food	0.9	7.7	8.3	14.1	14.7	28.6	29.6	5.3	4.0
Consumer durables	3.7	.1	.5	2.1	1.5	3.0	2.6	6.9	5.5
Producer durables	4.2	2.1	3.6	2.9	4.2	4.3	6.5	9.0	18.7
Nondurables less food and fuel	2.6	1.2	1.5	2.9	2.3	5.9	3.4	8.1	2.6
Food materials	3.2	7.4	5.8	16.8	11.1	39.0	23.9	14.7	7.6
Durable components	3.6	1.8	4.3	3.1	4.0	5.4	7.8	18.0	11.2
Durable materials	4.2	3.0	5.8	6.7	7.8	12.9	14.1	19.4	12.2
Nondurable materials less food and fuel	1.4	2.9	1.2	6.8	3.4	17.9	7.7	17.7	7.6
Construction materials	6.2	6.0	9.6	7.9	10.3	8.6	8.2	12.3	2.4

to have helped to reduce inflation rates in certain sectors. Therefore, a selective program of controls instead of a general price controls program seems preferable. However, these same sectors have exhibited the most rapid inflation since the terminating of controls. As a result their levels in September 1974 were at or above what they would have been in the absence of controls. This seems to support the view that price controls result in a temporary but not a permanent reduction in prices. However, if decontrol were selective and carefully managed, price bulges of the type recently experienced could be reduced. [4]

APPENDIX

--BEGIN MODEL SOPNEW

EQ: RUIEQ
RUI=1/RU

EQ: INTERESTIDENT
PMCR=(RMMTGNNS-RMMTGNNS(1)) /RMMTGNNS

EQ: EQ18
PCELEC=RO+R1*PSOP1300=R2*P0561+AFCELEC

EQ: ELECIDENTN
CPIELEC=CPIELEC(-1)*(1+PCELEC/100)

EQ: EQ12
PCSERV=L0+L1*PMCR+L2*((PAHERW(-2)+PAHERW(-3)+PAHERW(-4))/3)
+L3*((RUI(-3)+RUI(-4))/2)+L4*PCELEC+AFCSERV

EQ: SR4IN
CPISERV=CPISERV(-1)*(1+PCSERV/400)

EQ: EQ17
PWCONSTI=Q0+Q1*PWCONSTC+Q2*PSOP2400+ Q3*((HUSTS+HUSTS
(-1))/2)+AFWCONSTI

EQ: WPISOP2200IDENTN
WPISOP2200=WPISOP2200(-1)*(1+PWCONSTI/400)

EQ: WPISOP1300IDENIN
WPISOP1300=WPISOP1300(-1)*(1+PSOP1300/400)

EQ: WPIFUELIIDENIN
WPISOP2400=WPISOP2400(-1)*(1+PSOP2400/400)

EQ: WPIFUELFMNIDENTN
WPIFUELFMN=WPIFUELFMN(-1)*(1+PWFUELFMN/400)

EQ: CPIPETIDENIN
CPIPET=CPIPET(-1)*(1+PCPET/400)

--BEGIN MODEL SOPFOODN

EQ: WPISOP1100IDENTN
WPISOP1100=WPISOP1100(-1)*(1+PSOP1100/400).

EQ: EQ13
PSOP2100=M3+M4*((PSOP1100+PSOP1100(-1)+PSOP1100(-2))/3)+M5*
PSOP3112+AFWMFM

EQ: WPISOP2110IDENTN
WPISOP2100=WPISOP2100(-1)*(1+PSOP2100/400)

EQ: EQ9
PSOP3112=I0+I1*PSOP1100+I2*PSOP2100+I3*PWCONT+AFWCPF

EQ: FPFW4IN
WPISOP3112=WPISOP3112(-1)*(1+PSOP3112/400)

EQ: WPISOP3111IDENTN
WPISOP3111= WPISOP3111(01)*(1+PSOP311/400)

EQ: WPIFOODIDENTN
WPISOP3110=.15638*WPISOP3111+.84362*WPISOP3112

EQ: EQ10
PFDHOME=J0+J1*((PSOP3111+PSOP3111(-1))/2)+J2*((PSOP3112+PSOP
3112(-1))/2)+AFCFDHOME

EQ: FDHOMEIN
CPIFOODHOME=CPIFOODHOME(-1)*(1+PFDHOME/400)

EQ: EQ11
PCFAWH=K0+K1*((PSOP3112(-1)+PSOP3112(-2))/2)+K2*((PAHERW+PAHERW
(-1)+PAHERW(-2))/3)+K3*((RUI(-3)+RUI(-4))/2)+AFCFAWH

EQ: FAHR4IN
CPIFAWH=CPIFAWH(-1)*(1+PCFAWH/400)

EQ: CPIFDIDENTN2
CPIFOOD=.7879*CPIFOODHOME+.2121*CPIFAWH

--END MODEL SOPFOODN

--BEGIN MODEL SOPDURN

EQ: EQ4
PSOP2130=D0+D1*((PSOP1210+PSOP1210(-1))/2)+D2*((PAHEDG(-1)+
PAHEDG(-2))/2)+D3*UCAPFRBMATL(-1)+D4*PSOP2400+AFWMDM

EQ: D12W4IN
WPISOP2130=WPISOP2130(-1)*(1+PSOP2130/400)

EQ: EQ3
PSOP2140=C0+C1*((PSOP2130+PSOP2130(-1))/2)=G2*((UCAPFRBMATL(-3)
+UCAPFRBMATL(-4))/2)+C3*PSOP2400+C4*DUM3+AFWCMP

EQ: DI1W4IN
WPISOP2140=WPISOP2140(-1)*(1+PSOP2140/400)

EQ: EQ2
PSOP3130=B0+B1*PSOP2140+B2*PSOP2400+B3*PAHEDG(-4)+B4*RUI(-4)
+AFWDCG

EQ: DFW4IN
WPISOP3130=WPISOP3130(-1)*(1+PSOP3130/400)

EQ: EQ8
PSOP3200=H0+H1*((PSOP2140+PSOP2140(-1))/2)+H2*((PAHEDG+PAHEDG
(-1)+PAHEDG(-2))/3)+H3*PSOP2400+H4*ALLPH+AFWFPG

EQ: PDFW4IN
WPISOP3200=WPISOP3200(-1)*(1+PSOP3200/400)

EQ: EQ1
PCDG=A0+A1*PSOP3130+A2*((PAHERW(-3)+PAHERW(-4))/2)+A3*RUI(-4)
+AFCDG

EQ: DR4IN
CPIDG=CPIDG(-1)*(1+PCDG/400)

--END MODEL SOPDURN

--BEGIN MODEL SOPNONDURN

EQ: EQ7
PSOP2120=G0+G1*((PSOP1210+PSOP1210(-1))/2)+G2*PAHENG(-1)+G3*
((UCAPFRBMATL+UCAPFRBMATL(-1))/2)+AFWMNM

EQ: NIW4IN
WPISOP2120=WPISOP2120(-1)*(1+PSOP2120/400)

EQ: EQ6
PWNCXFFC=F0+F1*PSOP2120+F2*((PAHENG+PAHENG(-1))/2)+F3*((RUI
(-1)+RUI(-2)+RUI(-3))/3)+F4*PSOP2400+AFWNCXFFC

EQ: NFW4IN
WPINCXFFC=WPINCXFFC(-1)*(1+PWNCXFFC/400)

EQ: EQ5
PCNXFFC=E0+E1*((PWNCXFFC+PWNCXFFC(-1)+PWNCXFFC(-2))/3)+E2*
PAHERW+E3*((RUI(-1)+RUI(-2)+RUI(-3)+RUI(-4)/+AFCNXFFC

EQ: NR4IN
CPINXFFC=CPINXFFC(-1)*(1+PCNXFFC/400)

--END MODEL SOPNONDURN

--BEGIN MODEL EXTRAIDENTN

EQ: CPIIDENTN
CPI=.1765*CPIDG+.1776*CPIFOODHOME+.0398*CPIPET+.2056*CPIN
XFFC+.0478*CPIFAWH+.3528*CPISEPV

EQ: CPIXFSIDENTN
CPIXFU&S=.2904*CPIDG+.2924*CPIFOODHOME+.3385*CPINXFFC+
.0787*CPIFAWH

EQ: CPIXFUIDENTN
CPIXFU=.1838*CPIDG+.1849*CPIFOODHOME+.2141*CPINXFFC+.0498
*CPIFAWH+.3674*CPISERV

EQ: CPIXFU&FOIDENTN
CPIXFU&FO=.2401*CPIDG+.2798*CPINXFFC+.4801*CPISERV

EQ: WPISOP1220IDENTN
WPISOP1220=WPISOP1220(-1)*(1+PWCONSTC/400)

EQ: WPISOP2500IDENTN
WPISOP2500=WPISOP2500(-1)*(1+PWCONT/400)

EQ: WPISOP2600IDENTN
WPISOP2600=WPISOP2600(-1)*(1+PWSUPP/400)

EQ: WPIFCGNIDENTN
WPIFCGN=.41194*WPISOP3110+.26139*WPISOP3130+.32667*WPINCXFFC

EQ: WPIFCGNXFIDENTN
WPIFCGNXFQ=.5555*WPINCXFFC+.4445*WPISOP3130

EQ: WPIFIGIDENTN
WPISOP3000=.2208*WPISOP3200+.71814*WPIFCGN+.06106*WPIFUELFMN

EQ: WPIFTGXFUNIDENTN
WPIFTGXFUN=.76484*WPIFCGN+.23516*WPISOP3200

EQ: WPIMXFUNFOIDENTN
WPISOP2000XFU&FO=.3763*WPISOP2120+.3556*WPISOP2130+.2681*
WPISOP2140

EQ: WPIMXFUIDENTN
WPISOP2000XFU=.9033*WPISOP2000XFU&FO+.0967*WPISOP2100

EQ: WPIMCIDENTN
WPIMCN=.9006*WPISOP2000XFU+.0994*WPISOP2400

EQ: WPICNMIDENTN
WPISOP1210=WPISOP1210(-1)*(1+PSOP1210/400)

EQ: WPISOP1000MIDENTN
WPISOP1000=.244*WPISOP1210+.0722*WPISOP1300+.6603*WPISOP
1100+.0235*WPISOP1220

EQ: INTERMEDIDENTN
WPISOP2000=.6281*WPINCN+.1826*WPISOP2200+.0357*WPISOP
2500+.1536*WPISOP2600

EQ: WPIIDENTN
WPI= .11268*WPISOP1000+.44937*WPISOP2000+.43795*WPISOP3000

--END MODEL EXTRAIDENTN

Coefficients

R0	.1012	J2	0.6603	H1	0.5811
R1	0.0550	K0	-4.6528	H2	0.2997
R2	0.0394	K1	.38014	H3	0.05416
L0	-4.3592	K2	0.8969	H4	-0.7584
L1	0.3185	K3	14.7061	A0	-6.1104
L2	0.8783	D0	-16.4337	A1	.3824
L3	17.0011	D1	0.1374	A2	.9214
L4	0.5683	D2	0.5709	A3	11.9457
Q0	-7.3106	D3	18.4062	G0	-13.0292
Q1	.7537	D4	0.1478	G1	.3244
Q2	.1334	C0	-17.23	G2	.3805
Q3	5.2491	C1	0.4223	G3	13.6701
M3	.4873	C2	21.077	F0	-3.1000
M4	.3854	C3	0.0941	F1	0.1971
M5	.605	C4	-0.26128	F2	0.2902
I0	0.9287	B0	-2.7024	F3	15.0689
I1	0.3408	B1	.2288	F4	0.05529
I2	0.148	B2	.0765	E0	-1.7959
I3	0.21585	B3	.3389	E1	.6351
J0	0.6676	B4	8.7180	E2	.2574
J1	0.15765	H0	-0.1504	E3	9.4652

Summary Results

	Coefficient of Determination	Durbin-Watson
Food		
Intermediate materials	.53	1.72
Processed food	.89	1.92
Retail at home	.87	2.24
Retail away from home	.80	1.59
Services	.69	1.80
Electricity	.79	1.47
Durables		
Intermediate materials	.67	1.41
Components	.75	1.46
Consumer finished	.57	2.11
Producer finished	.81	1.86
Retail	.64	1.82
Nondurables less food and fuel		
Intermediate materials	.94	1.49
Finished	.81	2.21
Retail	.78	1.78
Construction Materials	.54	1.75

Variables	Definition	Adjustment Factors	Simple Annual Rates
CPI	Consumer Price Index		
WPI	Wholesale Price Index		
WPI3000	wholesale finished goods		
WPI2000	wholesale intermediate goods		
WPISOP2000xFU	wholesale intermediate materials and components for manufacturing		
WPI1000	wholesale crude goods		
WPI1100	crude foodstuffs and feedstuffs		PSOP1100
WPI2110	intermediate materials for food manufacturing	AFWMFM	PSOP2110
WPISOP3112	processed food	AFWCPF	PSOP3112
WPISOP3111	consumer crude food		PSOP3111
CPIFOODHOME	retail food at home	AFCFDHOME	PFDHOME
CPIFAWH	retail food away from home	AFCFAWH	PCFAWH
WPISOP1210	crude nonfood, nonfuel materials for manufacturing		PSOP1210
WPISOP2130	intermediate materials for durable manufacturing	AFWMDM	PSOP2130
WPISOP2140	components for manufacturing	AFWCMP	PSOP2140
WPISOP3130	consumer durable goods	AFWDCG	PSOP3130
WPISOP3200	producer finished goods	AFWFPG	PSOP3200
CPIDG	retail durable commodities	AFCDG	PCDG
WPISOP2120	intermediate materials less fuel for nondurable manufacturing	AFWMNM	PSOP2120
WPINCXFFC	consumer nondurable goods less food and fuel	AFWNCXFFC	PWNCXFFC
CPINXFFC	retail nondurable commodities less food and fuel	AFNCXFFC	PCNXFFC
WPISOP1300	crude fuel (coal, natural gas)		PSOP1300
WPISOP2400	intermediate petroleum products (electric power, natural gas, refined products)		PSOP2400
WPIFUELFMN	finished petroleum products (refined products, coal)		
CPIPET	retail petroleum products (gasoline, motor oil, heating oil)		
WPISOP1200	crude construction materials (sand, gravel, crushed stone)		PWCONSTC
WPISOP2200	intermediate construction materials	AFWCONSTI	PWCONSTI
WPISOP2500	containers		PWCONT
WPISOP2600	supplies		PWSUPP
CPISERV	retail services	AFCSERV	PCSERV
CPIXFU	all items less fuel		
CPIXFU&FO	total commodities less food		
CPIFOOD	total food		
CPIXFU&S	commodities less fuel and services		
CPIELEC	electricity	AFCELEC	PCELEC
CPIFOOD	total food		
WPIFCGN	consumer finished goods		
WPIFTGXFUN	total finished goods less fuel		
WPIFCGNXFO	total finished consumer goods less food		
WPIMCN	total intermediate materials and components for manufacturing plus fuel		
WPISOP2000XFU&FO	intermediate materials and components for manufacturing less food		
ARWNEWQ	average hourly earnings: retail and wholesale trade	AFAHERW	PAHERW
ADGNEWQ	average hourly earnings: durable manufacturing	AFAHEDG	PAHEDG
ANGNEWQ	average hourly earnings: nondurable manufacturing	AFAHENG	PAHENG
UCAPFRBMATL	capacity utilization - major materials industries		
RU	unemployment rate - civilian workers		
RUI	inverse of unemployment rate		
RMMTGNNS	mortgage rate - new homes		
PMCR	percentage change in mortgage rate		
HUSTS	housing starts		

NOTES

1. See Paul H. Earl, "A Disaggregate Analysis of the Economic Stabilization Program," paper presented at the Western Economic Association meetings, Las Vegas, Nev., June, 1974; John Kraft, "The Effectiveness of the Economic Stabilization Program: A Summary of the Evidence," in Analysis of Inflation, Paul H. Earl, ed. (Boston: D. C. Heath, forthcoming).

2. See Paul H. Earl, Inflation and the Structure of Industrial Prices (Boston, D. C. Heath, 1973); Otto Eckstein, ed., The Econometrics of Price Determination (Washington, D. C.: Federal Reserve Board, 1972); Otto Eckstein and Roger Brinner, "The Inflation Process in the United States," U. S. Congress Joint Economic Committee (Washington, D. C.: Government Printing Office, 1972); and Otto Eckstein and Gary Fromm, "The Price Equation," American Economic Review, 48 (December 1968), pp. 1159-83.

3. See Paul H. Earl, "A Disaggregate Analysis of the Economic Stabilization Program," op. cit.; and Charles Guy, John Kraft, and Blaine Roberts, "The Price Control Experiment: Short-Run Success and Long-Run Failure?" unpublished manuscript, 1973.

4. For further information see Arthur J. Alexander, "Prices and the Guideposts: The Effects of Government Persuasion on Individual Prices," The Review of Economics and Statistics 53 (February 1971), pp. 67-75; Barry Bosworth, "Phase II: the U. S. Experiment with an Incomes Policy," Brookings Papers on Economic Activity, no. 2 (1972), pp. 313-84; Barry Bosworth and John Farmer, "The Current Inflation: Malign Neglect?" Brookings Papers on Economic Activity, no. 1 (1973), pp. 263-84;

Office of the Federal Registrar, Economic Stabilization Code of Federal Regulations, Title 6, August 1971, March, June, and October 1972 (Washington, D. C.: Government Printing Office, 1971-72); Senate Committee on Banking, Housing and Urban Affairs, Subcommittee on Production and Stabilization, Statement of John T. Dunlop, February 6, 1974 (Washington, D. C.: Government Printing Office, 1974); Paul H. Earl, "The Effect of Controls on the Economy," an unpublished study prepared for the Cost of Living Council, February 1974;

Paul H. Earl, "An Analysis of the Economic Stabilization Program through Stages of Processing," paper presented at the Southern Economic Association meetings, Atlanta, November 1974 (mimeo); Paul H. Earl and Nancy E. Kennedy, "A Disaggregate Approach to Forecasting Prices," in Analysis of Inflation, edited by Paul H. Earl (Boston: D. C. Heath, forthcoming); Edgar Feige and Douglas Pearce, "The Wage-Price Control Experiment—Did It Work?" Challenge 16 (July-August 1973): 40-44;

Peter Fortune, "An Evaluation of Anti-Inflation Policies in the United States," New England Economic Review (January-February 1974),

pp. 1-27, 35-39; Robert J. Gordon, "Wage-Price Controls and the
Shifting Phillips Curve," Brookings Papers on Economic Activity, no. 2
(1972), pp. 385-430; Robert J. Gordon, "The Response of Wages and
Prices to the First Two Years of Controls," Brookings Papers on Economic Activity, no. 3 (1973), pp. 765-80;

John Kraft and Blaine Roberts, "The Social Costs and Benefits of
Incomes Policies," unpublished manuscript, 1973; George L. Perry,
"The Success of Anti-Inflation Policies in the United States," Journal
of Money, Credit, and Banking (February 1973), pp. 567-93; Jerry E.
Pohlman, Economics of Wage and Price Controls (Columbus, Ohio, Grid,
1972); William Poole, "Wage-Price Controls: Where Do We Go from
Here?" Brookings Papers on Economic Activity, no. 1 (1973), pp. 285-
302;

William Poole, "An Evaluation of Anti-Inflation Policies in the
United States—Comment," New England Economic Review (January-
February 1974), pp. 28-34; Joel Popkin, "Prices in 1972: An Analysis
of Changes during Phase 2," Monthly Labor Review 96 (February 1973):
16-23; Joel Popkin, "Consumer and Wholesale Prices in a Model of
Price Behavior by Stages of Processing," Review of Economics and
Statistics (forthcoming); Joel Popkin, "Commodity Prices and the U.S.
Price Level," Brookings Papers on Economic Activity, no. 1 (1974),
pp. 249-60.

9

WAGE AND PRICE CONTROLS: SUCCESS OR FAILURE?

John Kraft

Blaine Roberts

Whether the wage and price controls program was a success or a failure is not a simple question, and the controversy surrounding the first formal peacetime controls program is anything but settled. One certainty is that many lessons, both good and bad, have been learned from the experience. However, the actual success or failure of the program is measured in terms of how well the program reduced inflationary wage and price movements.

The Economic Stabilization Program attempted to fight inflation at the microeconomic level of activity via the establishment of certain rules and guidelines. These procedures, whether general or industry specific, attempted to control price and wage increases at the firm level. The specific rules as designed for particular industries and firms were somewhat successful in controlling the price and wage increases of the groups they were specifically targeted for. For example, inflationary wage settlements in the aircraft industry and inflationary price increases in certain segments of the steel industry were effectively controlled. However, the final test of the success or failure of the controls program does not rest with how well the program implemented its many rules and procedures but rather how it affected the movements of aggregate wages and prices.

This chapter reviews the evidence of recent studies of the behavior of aggregate wages and prices during the period of wage and price controls. The studies reviewed are grouped into three categories: preliminary evaluations of Phase I (the freeze) and Phase II; complete evaluations of Phases I and II; and later evaluations of Phases I and II and beyond. This list is by no means complete, but is representative of the empirical evaluations of the Economic Stabilization Program. Studies by the following authors are reviewed:

Authors	Sector Studied
A. Bradley Askin and John Kraft[1]	private nonfarm
Robert J. Gordon[2]	private nonfarm
U. S. Congress, Joint Economic Committee[3]	private economy
A. Bradley Askin and John Kraft[4]	private nonfarm
Arthur Kraft, John Kraft, and Blaine Roberts[5]	manufacturing
Robert F. Lanzillotti and Blaine Roberts[6]	private economy
Joel Popkin[7]	private economy
Charles Guy, John Kraft, and Blaine Roberts[8]	sixteen manufacturing industries
Edgar Feige and Douglas Pearce[9]	private economy
George de Menil[10]	business nonfarm
Barry Bosworth[11]	private economy
Charles Guy, John Kraft, and Blaine Roberts[12]	stages of processing

REVIEW OF THE EVIDENCE

In reviewing each study we will identify the sector wage and price variable, the form of the variables, the method of estimation, and the direct and total impact of wages and prices annually.

Preliminary Evaluation of Phase II

Askin and Kraft, "Similarities and Differences among Three Models of the Inflation Process." This study examines the impact of controls on the private, nonfarm economy from 1971:3 to 1972:4 by three different functional models of wage and price equations, one using current period and lags, another estimated with polynomial distributed lags, and the last a weighted lag form. The data is all in quarterly form, and all three studies have the same wage and price variables. The wage variable is the index of average hourly earnings of production workers for the private, nonfarm economy, adjusted for overtime and interindustry employment shifts. The price variable is the implicit GNP deflator for the private, nonfarm economy. The estimated impact of controls on prices and wages is only calculated as a direct annual percentage-point impact for each of the three models.

direct price impact: -1.24 to +1.96
direct wage impact: -0.92 to +1.08

Gordon, "Wage-Price Controls and the Shifting Phillips Curve." The
Gordon study is a preliminary evaluation of the impact of controls on
the private nonfarm sector by comparing the actual performance of wages
and prices during the control period with the performance predicted by
the model in simulations from 1971:3 through 1972:2. The price variable
is the implicit GNP deflator for the private nonfarm economy, and the
wage variable is the index of average hourly earnings of production
workers for the private nonfarm economy, adjusted for overtime and
interindustry shifts. The model is estimated using polynomial distributed
lags. The direct and total annual percentage-point impacts are

Direct price impact	-1.47
Direct wage impact	-0.48
Total price impact	-1.85
Total wage impact	-0.68

U.S. Congress Joint Economic Committee, "Price and Wage Controls:
Evaluation of a Year's Experience." The Joint Economic Committee
study is a descriptive evaluation of controls covering the period from
1971:3 through 1972:3. The conclusions of the report were, "Wage
controls were more effective than price controls; the price controls have
failed to adequately hold down prices." (p. 5) Some selected measures
of wages and prices for the 1971:3-1972:3 period are reported in percentage change as follows:

Hourly compensation for private, nonfarm economy	6.1 percent
Consumer Price Index	3.4 percent

The target for wages and prices was

Wages hourly compensation	5.5 percent
Consumer prices	2.5 percent

Evaluation of Phase II

Askin and Kraft, Econometric Wage and Price Models. This study is an
expanded version of the above-mentioned Askin and Kraft Preliminary
Evaluation of Phase II, using three models of the private nonfarm
economy in an attempt to ascertain the impact of the Economic Stabilization Program on the index of average hourly earnings for the private

nonfarm sector, adjusted for overtime and interindustry shifts, and the implicit price deflator for the private, nonfarm economy. The models are quarterly models, using three specifications; lags, polynomial distributed lags, and weighted lags. The measured annual percentage-point impacts are

Direct price impact	-1.28 to 1.96
Direct wage impact	-0.48 to +1.08
Total price impact	-1.20 to -2.60
Total wage impact	-1.49 to +0.10

Kraft, Kraft, and Roberts, "An Alternative to Wage and Price Controls."
The Kraft, Kraft, and Roberts study examines the impact of controls on the manufacturing sector for the 1971:3-1972:4 period. The dependent variable of the wage equation is the four-quarter rate of change in the fixed weight gross wage index. The price variable is the four-quarter rate of change in the weighted average of output prices for 16 manufacturing industries. The output prices for each two-digit SIC code[13] are weighted by the 1958 value of shipments. The wage and price equation is adjusted for autocorrelation using a nonlinear estimation procedure and a Hildreth-Lu search as a check. The estimated annual percentage-point impacts are as follows:

Direct price impact	+0.37
Direct wage impact	+1.32
Total price impact	+1.79
Total wage impact	+1.80

Lanzillotti and Roberts, "The Legacy of Phase II Price Controls." This study is a descriptive evaluation of Phase II. It presents no impact measures but concentrates on an evaluation of the benefits and costs of controls with an estimated benefit-cost ratio of between 11.7 and 17.5 for Phase II. It concludes that the six quarters of controls resulted in an average reduction in the annual rate of inflation of 2 percent points and a minimal influence on wages.

Popkin, "Prices in 1972: An Analysis of Changes during Phase II."
The Popkin paper is a descriptive analysis of prices during Phase II. Prices for most major commodities in the Consumer Price Index and the Wholesale Price Index rose at a slower rate in 1972 than in the first eight months of 1971. The WPI rose 5.2 percent in the eight months prior to August 1971 and 5.3 percent in the first sixteen months of controls. The CPI, all items, compared on the same basis, rose 3.8 percent in the precontrols period and 3.2 percent in the controls period.

Guy, Kraft, and Roberts, "Wage and Price Controls: An Industrial Examination." This study estimates wage, price, and profit-margin equations
for 16 manufacturing industries. The variables are constructed in four-
quarter rates of change, and the equations are estimated with corrections
for autocorrelation. The wage variable is average hourly earnings and
the price variable is an index of output prices.[14] The study only estimates the direct impact of the controls program. For the economy the
coefficients are not reported. In many instances the impact is insignificant. A summary of the significant direct impact is given in Table 9.1.

Feige and Pearce "The Wage-Price Control Experiment—Did It Work?"
This study is an evaluation of the impact of controls on the private
economy. Using Box Jenkins time series techniques, Feige and Pearce
estimate the impact of the controls program. They conclude that on the
basis of past variations in the rate of change in the CPI, the rate of
change in the index would have slowed by exactly the amount it did,
giving a zero impact for the controls program. The average change in
the WPI, on this basis, was 1.4 percent higher and the average change
in wages was reduced by .8 percent. If the December figures for the
WPI are omitted, the actual average change for the 15 months from
September 1971 to November 1972 is 4.2 percent, while the model
predicts 4 percent for the same period, thus changing the impact on the
WPI to +.2 percent. Thus, on the basis of how each series moved
independently in the past, Feige and Pearce conclude that the slowdown
in prices would have occurred anyway, whereas the slowdown for wages
would not have occurred.

DeMenil, "Aggregate Price Dynamics." de Menil estimates a dynamic
aggregate price equation. The dependent variable is the first difference
of the logarithm of a constructed index of the price of gross output in
private business non-farm sector. In testing for the direct impact of
controls de Menil estimated a 1.4 percent annual average reduction in
price for the entire period. The average for Freeze I is 2.2 percent and
for Phase II is 1.0 percent.

Evaluation of Phase III

Bosworth, "The Inflation Problem during Phase III." Bosworth concluded
that the Phase III inflation was aptly labeled a commodity inflation;
that the inflation of 1973 represented the costs of previous mistakes;
and that the inflation was primarily a function of bottlenecks and
commodity inflation which had its roots in Phase II.

TABLE 9.1

Significant Direct Impact of Price Controls

	Prices		Wages		Profit Margins	
	Positive	Negative	Positive	Negative	Positive	Negative
SIC	23	21	20	23	26	22
equations	24		25	24	28	371
	26		26	36	30	
	331		32		331	
			331			
			333			

Source: Compiled by the author.

Guy, Kraft, and Roberts, "The Determination of Wages and Prices through Stages of Processing." This is a stage-of-processing model estimated on a monthly basis. The variables are constructed as a ratio of the current value to a four-quarter moving average. The model computes direct and total impacts of controls and differentiates between Phase II and Phase III direct impacts. In all cases the program was less effective in Phase II than Phase III. This did not affect farm products, since they were exempt in Phase II. It can be generally concluded that the effects of controls are mixed for the entire period but generally weaker in Phase III, as commodity inflation and bottlenecks proved.

SUMMARY

An examination of this evidence should generally result in a no-decision conclusion; the problems of measurement and specification have prevented a consensus opinion. One conclusion that can be drawn is that in Phase II, wages in general were pushed up by controls or held down to a lesser extent than prices. This evidence would indicate a redistribution of income towards workers in the form of higher real incomes. This was not true of Phase III, where the balance swung back to prices. Whether controls ever had a lasting impact or whether they had any impact at all will probably not be decided for some years to come.

88888

777

NOTES

1. "Similarities and Differences among Three Models of the Inflation Process, with a Preliminary Evaluation of Controls." The Southern Economic Journal 40, no. 1 (July 1974): 21-38.

2. "Wage-Price Controls and the Shifting Phillips Curve," Brookings Papers on Economic Activity, no. 2 (1972) pp. 385-430.

3. "Price and Wage Controls: Evaluation of a Year's Experience," December 14, 1972 (Washington, D.C.: Government Printing Office, 1972).

₂ 4. Econometric Wage and Price Models (Lexington, Mass.: D. C. Heath, 1974).

5. "An Alternative to Wage and Price Controls," in Wage and Price Controls: The U.S. Experiment (New York: Praeger Publishers, 1975).

6. "The Legacy of Phase II Price Controls," American Economic Review 64, no. 2, (May 1974): 82-87.

7. "Prices in 1972: An Analysis of Changes during Phase II," Monthly Labor Review 96 (February 1973): 16-23.

8. "Wage and Price Controls: An Industrial Examination," in Wage and Price Controls: The U.S. Experiment (New York: Praeger Publishers, 1975).

9. "The Wage-Price Control Experiment—Did it Work?" Challenge 16 (July-August 1973): 40-44.

10. "Aggregate Price Dynamics," The Review of Economics and Statistics 56, no. 2, (May 1974): 129-40.

11. "The Inflation Problem during Phase III," American Economic Review 64, no. 2 (May 1974): 93-99.

12. "The Determination of Wages and Prices through Stages of Processing," working paper, 1974. (mimeo)

13. Constructed in Guy, Kraft, and Roberts, "Wage and Price Controls: And Industrial Examination," op. cit., following the procedure established by Otto Eckstein and David Wyss, "Industry Price Equations," The Econometrics of Price Determiation/Conference (Washington, D.C.: Board of Governors, Federal Reserve System, 1972).

14. For a discussion of this index, see Kraft, Kraft, and Roberts, op. cit.

ABOUT THE CONTRIBUTORS

A. BRADLEY ASKIN is Assistant Professor in the Graduate School of Administration at the University of California at Irvine. Currently he is on academic leave as Economist and Federal Faculty Fellow at the Federal Energy Administration. Prior to accepting this fellowship he served as a consultant to the Rand Corporation and to the Price Commission. He is coauthor of Econometric Wage and Price Models (D. C. Heath). Dr. Askin received a Ph. D. in economics from the Massachusetts Institute of Technology.

PAUL EARL is Assistant Professor in the Department of Economics at Georgetown University and a consultant to Data Resources, Inc. During Phases III and IV Dr. Earl worked as a consultant to the Cost of Living Council. He is the author of Inflation and the Structure of Industrial Prices.

CHARLES GUY is an economist with the Council on Wage and Price Stability. During the Economic Stabilization Program he was an economist with the Price Commission and the Cost of Living Council. He has a Ph. D. from the University of Florida.

SIDNEY L. JONES is Deputy Assistant to the President and Deputy to the Counselor to the President for Economic Policy. From June 1973 to June 1974, Dr. Jones was Assistant Secretary of Commerce for Economic Affairs in the U. S. Department of Commerce.

ARTHUR KRAFT is Professor of Quantitative Methods at Ohio University. Currently he is on academic leave as an economist and as Federal Faculty Fellow at the Social Security Administration. He received his Ph. D. in economics from the State Univesity of New York at Buffalo.

JOHN KRAFT is Director of Econometric Modeling and Research with the Federal Energy Administration. Dr. Kraft formerly served as a Brookings Economic Policy Fellow at the Price Commission and Director of Analytical Studies at the Cost of Living Council. He has a Ph. D. from the University of Pittsburgh.

DANIEL J. B. MITCHELL is Associate Professor, Graduate School of Management, University of California, Los Angeles. During Phase II of the Economic Stabilization Program he was Chief Economist of the Pay Board. He returned to UCLA in 1973 after a brief tour with the Brookings Institution. Dr. Mitchell has written extensively in the area of labor economics and incomes policy. He has a Ph. D. from the Massachusetts Institute of Technology in economics.

JERRY E. POHLMAN is an economist with Arthur Young & Company. He formerly served as an economist with the Cost of Living Council and the Price Commission. Before that he was a professor at the State University of New York at Buffalo.

BLAINE ROBERTS is Associate Professor of Economics at the University of Florida. During Phase II he was Deputy Director of Price Analysis at the Price Commission. From February 1973 to September 1973 he was with the Brookings Institution. He has a Ph. D. in economics from Iowa State University.

JEROME M. STALLER is Senior Staff Economist in the Office of Policy Development, U. S. Department of Labor. He was previously Director of Wage Analysis at the Cost of Living Council and a labor economist with the Pay Board. Dr. Staller taught at Pennsylvania State University from 1968-74. He received his B.A., M.A., and Ph. D. from Temple University.

LOREN M. SOLNICK is Assistant Professor of Human Resource Management at the State University of New York at Albany. Previously he has served as a labor economist with both the Cost of Living Council and the U. S. Department of Labor and has been on the faculty of Claremont Men's College. Dr. Solnick has a B.A. in economics from City College of New York and holds an M.S. and Ph. D. from Cornell University.

PERSPECTIVES ON TAX REFORM: Death Taxes,
Tax Loopholes, and the Value Added Tax

> Richard E. Wagner, Roger A.
> Freeman, Charles E. McClure, Jr.,
> Norman B. Ture, and Eric Schiff

REVENUE SHARING: Legal and Policy Analysis

> Otto G. Stoltz

THE PROPERTY TAX AND ALTERNATIVE LOCAL TAXES

> Larry D. Schroeder and
> David L. Sjoquist

INCOME DISTRIBUTION POLICIES AND
ECONOMIC GROWTH IN SEMI-INDUSTRIALIZED
COUNTRIES

> Robert E. Looney